Violence and the Schools:
A Collection

Edited By
Phillip Harris

IRI/Skylight Publishing, Inc.
Palatine, Illinois

Violence and the Schools: A Collection
First Printing

Published by IRI/Skylight Publishing, Inc.
200 E. Wood Street, Suite 274
Palatine, Illinois 60067
Phone 800-348-4474, 708-991-6300
FAX 708-991-6420

Creative Director: Robin Fogarty
Editors: Liesl Banks-Stiegman, Heidi Ray, Amy Wolgemuth
Type Compositor: Donna Ramirez
Book Designers: Michael Melasi, Bruce Leckie
Production Coordinators: David Stockman, Amy Behrens

Library of Congress Catalog Number 94-78545

Printed in the United States of America
ISBN 0-932935-80-X

1254-9-94

Table of Contents

Introduction

Violence and the Schools: A Collection

On a recent visit to a middle school, I walked into a surprising situation. The principal was in a serious dilemma—she was deciding whether or not to continue her career. I asked her why she would even consider leaving a school she was so devoted to, and she explained. The previous week, a student had been sent to her office over an infraction of the rules. When she discussed the violation with the young man, he exploded. He knocked things off her desk, swiped at the books on her book cases, and demolished her wall hangings. Fortunately, he ran out of the office before harming the principal. But he wreaked havoc as he ran down the hallway.

The principal called 911. The police arrived and subsequently subdued the student. They called the young man's father and asked him to come for his son, but he said that he didn't have time. Left with no other choice, the police went to the father's workplace, picked him up, and took him to the school. Not surprisingly, the father became enraged. This caused the principal to fear for her safety and to question all the time, energy, and commitment needed to continue in her career.

Unfortunately, incidents like this one are happening every day in our schools. This particular scenario occurred in a midwestern community of 40,000. Violence is no longer just an inner-city problem. Acts of violence reported each day in our public schools mirror the same senseless acts perpetrated daily in society. Those who believe that violence is not a school problem deny reality.

Violent behavior encroaches on the school in much the same manner as it does in the workplace. Corporate America is fast becoming aware of the problem. Violence in the schools is exceeded only by violence in the workplace. Those in the work force must come to terms with the problem in the same manner as teachers and administrators do in the schools. Dealing with violence in the workplace raises the cost of doing business. Likewise, for schools, stopping violence adds to the expense of education. In the workplace, funds to combat violence will be generated from the private sector; schools, however, will be expected to find their own resources to deal with the problem.

The general public doesn't expect corporate America to deal with what has been termed "random acts of violence." They *do* expect public education to deal with the violence in the schools. Yet it is clear that "school solutions" are "community solutions." The school is simply a microcosm of the community. It is not a case of violence *in* the schools, but one of violence *and* the schools. Remedies will be limited by what the community is willing and able to support.

Health professionals, a voice from the community, see school violence as a public health issue. They ask: Are we willing to label violence a public health issue? Are we willing to commit resources and form school-community partnerships to find solutions? Solutions that fail to approach the problem from the community perspective will be superficial at best. If violence and the schools is not viewed as a community problem, critics will claim that the problem is in the schools' lack of discipline, lack of standards, and lack of responsible school policy.

The problem will not disappear. The message of this collection is that the schools, along with other social agencies and institutions, must work for a solution. Educators cannot combat this problem by themselves, and they need not absorb the guilt with every act of senseless violence.

This collection is organized around startling and disturbing statistics that paint a frightening picture. An understanding of the real problem is essential to focus national attention. The challenge to us all is to take an honest look and realize it is our problem and we must all commit our energies to it.

This collection offers the reader the opportunity to understand the violence problem and to reflect on what others are saying and doing about violence. Four comprehensive sections provide a manageable overview of the problem of "violence and the schools": Section 1: Attention: Guns, Gangs, and Grades; Section 2: Prevention: People, Policies, and Programs; Section 3: Intervention: Crisis, Communication, and Commitment; and Section 4: Honorable Mention: Agencies, Bureaus, and Coalitions.

Attention: Guns, Gangs, and Grades

T he data on incidents of violence in schools are alarming. Why is violence occurring? Who are the perpetrators and victims? What is happening to that once safe haven where students and teachers could step away from the problems of the streets and focus on educational issues and the quest for learning and creating a better world? Disruptive students have been a part of the educational environment for forty years. Violent students, however, are a recent phenomenon, and few educators are prepared to deal with them.

Headlines, articles, journals, magazines, and books about violence scream for our attention, presenting a problem that can no longer be ignored. These stories clearly demonstrate that we must act now. We cannot wait for someone else to devise a plan of action. Educators nationwide are responding in positive and constructive ways to the violence occurring daily in our nation's schools.

Section One includes articles that heighten our awareness. The first piece is excerpted from *Hot Topics: Usable Research, Reducing School Violence,* a publication created by the South-Eastern Regional Vision for Education. This excerpt by Stephanie Kadel and Joseph Follman comprises startling statistics that demonstrate how serious the problem has become. Next, Jessica Portner reports on the government's attempts to combat youth violence and provides insight into the opinions of educators.

The last three articles in this section point out that the violence problem in our public schools is very real and has to be addressed from all possible directions if we are to see the trend reversed. Anthony Moriarty and Thomas Fleming provide information on how gangs start and show that school violence is not only an urban problem. Wally Bowen explores the media influence on violence and our schools—how brutality is glamorized by movies, news programs, and sporting events. And Stephanie Kadel and Joseph Follman discuss the emotional and behavioral effects that violence has on the lives of students and teachers as well as the legal ramifications of violence for schools.

Introduction

by Stephanie Kadel and Joseph Follman

No school—whether small or large; elementary, middle, or high; poor or rich; urban, rural, or suburban—is immune from violence. Crime and violence pervade schools across the nation. How bad is the problem?

• Nearly three million crimes occur on or near schools every year; 16,000 take place each day, or one every six seconds (Morganthau et al., 1992).

• Nationwide, between September 1986 and June 1990, at least 75 people were killed with guns at school, over 200 were severely wounded by guns, and at least 242 were held hostage at school by gun-wielding assailants (Gaustad, 1991).

• Homicide is the leading cause of death among African-American males aged 15 to 19 years and the second leading cause of death for all youth (Lawton, 1992).

• Of 546 teenagers asked about violence they had seen at school, 83 percent had witnessed fighting, 16 percent had seen students assault teachers, 20 percent had seen a student pull a knife on someone, and 7 percent had witnessed someone being threatened with a gun (Peterson, 1992).

• In a recent study, forty-three percent of inner-city youth age 7-19 said they had witnessed a homicide (Morganthau et al., 1992).

• Approximately 97 percent of young rape victims in a survey of "Who's Who Among High School Students" knew their attackers; only 31 percent of victims reported the rape to the police (Lacy, 1993).

From *Hot Topics: Usable Research, Reducing School Violence,* the SouthEastern Regional Vision for Education, 1993, p. vii. Reprinted with permission.

• A 1991 survey of Florida students found that 24 percent had carried a weapon in the previous 30 days (Florida Department of Education, 1992).

• Every school day, 160,000 students skip classes because they fear physical harm, and 6,250 teachers are physically attacked (National Education Association, 1993).

Knowing that violence in schools is merely a reflection of violence in our society is of little comfort to teachers and administrators. Acts of violence disrupt the normal functioning of a school, and fear of violence prevents students and teachers from concentrating on meaningful learning and teaching. Money that should be spent on instructional materials, staff development, and other educational necessities is spent on security. Forced to prepare for the worst, schools are taking measures to discourage violence on school grounds as well as in surrounding communities.

REFERENCES

Florida Department of Education. (1992). *1991 Florida youth risk behavior survey report.* Tallahassee, FL: Prevention Center.

Gaustad, J. (1991). Schools respond to gangs and violence [Special issue]. *Oregon School Study Council (OSSC) Bulletin, 34*(9).

Lacy, M. (1993, January 25). Date rape: A fear many teens live with. *Tallahassee Democrat,* 15D.

Lawton, M. (1992, June 17). Warning of growing public-health crisis, journal examines teenage gun violence. *Education Week,* 14.

Morganthau, T., Annin, P., McCormick, J., Wingert, P., Foote, D., Manly, H., & King, P. (1992, March 9). It's not just New York...Big cities, small towns: More and more guns in younger and younger hands. *Newsweek,* 25–26, 29.

National Education Association. (1993, January 25). Every school day... *Time,* 23.

Peterson, K. (1992, May 20). Violence becomes part of school life. *USA Today,* D-1.

Educators Keeping Eye on Measures Designed to Combat Youth Violence

by Jessica Portner

Faced with a disturbing number of student crimes and gun incidents, and limited security budgets with which to address such problems, educators are scrutinizing a batch of youth-related-crime legislation making its way through Congress.

Late last month, the House Subcommittee on Select Education and Civil Rights approved the "safe and drug-free schools and communities act," which was attached last week to a bill reauthorizing the Elementary and Secondary Education Act.

The measure calls for grants to public schools to set up violence-prevention programs and build anti-crime coalitions, and would provide technical assistance to school districts to combat juvenile crime and drug use. Secretary of Education Richard W. Riley said the Administration will ask for $660 million for the program in next year's budget.

Because the E.S.E.A. will not be passed late in the year, the House Subcommittee on Elementary, Secondary, and Vocational Education last week also approved a separate, one-year safe-schools bill. It would authorize $50 million this year, although the Education Department budget includes only $20 million.

Under that bill, HR 3455, districts with high rates of violence would be eligible to apply for grants this year to prevent

From *Education Week*, vol. 13, no. 20, p. 21, Feb. 9, 1994. Reprinted with permission.

crime and improve security on school grounds. The full Education and Labor committee is expected to consider the measure this week; the Senate last week voted to attach a similar provision to the Administration's proposed "goals 2000: educate America act."

> **We have to reduce the carnage in our schools, and the Administration is in sync with us.**

In addition, the anti-crime bill that passed the Senate last fall would authorize $300 million for a three-year grant program for schools to develop alternative punishments for youth offenders, purchase metal detectors, or fund other crime-prevention efforts. The House Judiciary Committee is considering a similar measure.

MIXED REACTION

The federal pitch for school safety reached a crescendo last month when President Clinton pledged in his State of the Union Message to offer solutions to the problem of violent crime.

So far, educators generally have applauded the Administration's leadership on the issue.

"We have to reduce the carnage in our schools, and the Administration is in sync with us," said Timothy J. Dyer, the executive director of the National Association of Secondary School Principals.

"What the Administration has done is put school safety on the education agenda," added Ronald D. Stephens, the executive director of the National School Safety Center.

But many educators find some of the Administration's approach problematic.

Many school leaders object to the Administration's request that no more than 33 percent of the money for the safe-schools program be used for metal detectors.

"I understand that when your house is burning down you don't start remodeling the kitchen, you put out the fire," said John Cole, the president of the Texas Federation of Teachers. "But spending money on security systems is the wrong response to the problem."

President Clinton's call to stiffen penalties for repeat offenders also rankled some school-safety experts.

"Three strikes, and you're out? Is our whole response [to violence] going to be based on cute phrases?" asked Peter Blauvelt, the director of school security for Prince George's County, Md., district in the Washington suburbs.

Chancellor Ramon C. Cortines of the New York City schools charged that "the Administration is not taking the school-security issue seriously," which he said is evidenced by the proposed level of federal funding. Prevention also should be emphasized more, he said.

> **We can't talk about conflict resolution in the classroom when people are shooting each other in traffic.**

"You've got kids in the community ready to explode because of what's going on inside them," Mr. Cortines said.

Henry Fraind, the assistant superintendent of the Dade County, Fla., schools, said that "easy access to firearms" is responsible for most of the bloodshed in public schools and that until the government puts stricter limits on gun purchases, nothing will change.

"We can't talk about conflict resolution in the classroom when people are shooting each other in traffic," he said.

Some said one problem with the Administration's strategy is that most schools, legislators, and school policymakers lack a uniform definition of school violence, and schools often do not keep adequate records of violent incidents.

Many educators also advocate creation of a national data base so that schools can share information on juvenile offenders.

Over all, educators hope the funding for school-safety measures will match federal leaders' tough talk on the issue.

"The funding in the [House] school-safety bill is pretty inadequate considering the rhetorical attention being given the problem," said Michael Casserly, the executive director of the Council of the Great City Schools. "But Congress has never come so close before."

Meanwhile, as the legislation moves through Congress, Administration officials are busy developing a comprehensive strategy to help educators and others address school violence.

TASK FORCE AT WORK

The Administration's working group on school violence, made up of officials from the Education, Justice, and Health and Human Services departments, is expected to publish its recommendations this spring.

The report will cover five broad areas and offer guidance to educators on how to develop safe-schools policies, said William Modzeleski, the director of drug planning and outreach for the Education Department and a member of the task force.

Mr. Modzeleski said in an interview last week that the report will call on schools to develop safety plans and to organize training for students in managing conflict.

He said mentoring programs and information sharing should be elements of a successful school-safety plan, but warned against relying too heavily on any one of these areas.

"School security is one leg of this many-legged creature," Mr. Modzeleski said.

He also noted that the impact of such programs is limited by larger societal problems, as the crime in schools reflects that in society.

"Schools can be buffers, but they can't buffer it all out," he said.

Youth Gangs Aren't Just a Big-City Problem Anymore

by Anthony Moriarty and Thomas W. Fleming

T ime was, suburban school executives could simply dismiss talk of Crips and Bloods, of Vice Lords and Black Gangster Disciples. Gangs, they reasoned, were a problem only urban school systems faced.

No more. Ronald Stephens, executive director of the National School Safety Center in Encino, Calif., underscores what many suburban school officials and police officers already know: Youth gangs are no longer the exclusive problem of large metropolitan areas. Suburban communities—with their lucrative drug markets—are vulnerable to this problem, too.

> **Youth gangs are no longer the exclusive problem of large metropolitan areas.**

Suburban school officials who battle gangs by trying to pinpoint the "outsiders" are looking in the wrong direction, though. Here in Park Forest, Ill. (a suburb of Chicago), we've found that gangs typically don't invade suburban schools from the outside, sending out gang members to recruit new members and extending their territory. Instead, gangs grow up almost spontaneously within schools, by default rather than by design. And the catalysts are most likely to be transfer students from the city, marginally acquainted with gang paraphernalia and desperately trying to impress their new peers.

From *The Executive Educator*, vol. 12, no. 7, p. 13–16, July 1990. Reprinted with permission.

SEEKING A BETTER LIFE

Call it the newcomer syndrome. With their promise of safety
and economic opportunity, the suburbs around most large cities have become a powerful attraction for many city residents.
Often, in fact, inner-city parents move their families to the suburbs or send their children to live with a grandparent or other
relative in a suburban community to escape urban problems.
Determined to protect their youngsters from the influences of
street gangs and to give their youngsters a better education,
these parents will break up their families so their children can
live in the safer suburbs.

In our experience, though, inner-city youngsters who enter
a suburban school system sometimes find themselves at a significant disadvantage, both academically and socially. Their
families might not have the incomes many suburban families
do, and the schools they've attended might not have prepared
them to cope with the academic demands of a comprehensive
suburban high school. In many cases, they can't excel on the
athletic field, either. Lacking the skill, experience, and coaching
of many of their suburban counterparts, many newcomers
don't make the team and have little other opportunity to play.

These students are in an extremely precarious position.
Like all teenagers, they want their peers to accept or recognize
them—and they'll find a means of acceptance one way or another. Given no other opportunity to feel adequate—to feel like
they belong—these students are likely to revert to the trappings
of "the old neighborhood." For some, this means exploiting the
knowledge of gang language and symbols they recognize from
the city.

Put another way, these inner-city youngsters know why
they have been sent to the suburbs: to avoid gangs and get a better education. When that so-called "better" education becomes
a major source of intimidation, however, gangs become
attractive.

And this raises a second problem: Marginal students who
are established residents of the suburban community are likely
to be intrigued by the new student who flaunts gang symbols.
Most schools have a group of students who remain on the pe-
riphery of school life. Limited in both academic and athletic
ability, these kids spend a lot of time hanging out and looking

for things to do—and they are vulnerable to whatever influence comes their way. An alleged gang member will certainly be an attraction to them, if only as an antidote to their boredom.

With a group of youngsters gathering around, the displaced student from the city gains a sense of importance and leadership status that suburban life might otherwise deny him—status higher than he could have achieved in a city gang. Suddenly, he begins to realize that suburban life is not so bad after all. He can find power within the school walls, and he does not need to meet the school's expectations to satisfy his own needs.

> **All suburban schools, regardless of their racial or ethnic populations, are vulnerable to gangs.**

To succeed, any plan for gang prevention must address both the student who serves as the nucleus of a suburban gang and those students who are drawn to the gang life.

A 10-STEP PLAN

What might a gang-prevention plan look like? We've identified 10 strategies for addressing the problems of gang influence in suburban schools, and we're confident that if schools adopt these strategies, they'll go a long way toward making themselves gang-proof. In fact, schools that follow these strategies will become the one place where young people can be guaranteed safety and full protection from a problem that has plagued our society for too long. Here are our 10 gang-prevention strategies.

1. Be honest. Admit to the potential for problems in your school. All suburban schools, regardless of their racial or ethnic populations, are vulnerable to gangs. Denying this fact simply increases your vulnerability. Some school executives put a higher priority on maintaining a squeaky-clean reputation with the public than on preventing gangs. But this narrow view of community relations overlooks the fact that the community can be the school's greatest ally.

In our experience, most communities will judge school officials as perceptive and enlightened if they address the issue of suburban gangs before their schools have a problem. School officials also are more likely to obtain community support for their antigang efforts if they accurately apprise community leaders about the seriousness of the phenomenon before any problem occurs. Community leadership is a powerful force. The school official who doesn't play straight with community leaders is in serious trouble.

2. Get smart. School executives need to become aware of the myriad of gang symbols and paraphernalia. Example: Street gangs have a language all their own, and they'll test your ability to understand it. The biggest victory a young gang member can score in a school is to walk by the principal flaunting gang colors—and come away unscathed. Such ignorance sends a clear message: It tells gang members your school is vulnerable to their territorial battles.

> **Let gang members know they must leave their colors at the door if they are to come to your school.**

School policies should state clearly that the school will not tolerate gang symbols, paraphernalia, or any communication in gang language. (You might even recommend adopting a policy that makes any display of gang colors in the school cause for expulsion, although it probably would be prudent to consult with the school attorney before you do.) Such policies will present serious problems for gang members intent on territorial marking, recruitment, and intimidation. They let gang members know they must leave their colors at the door if they are to come to your school.

3. Identify your school's leaders, and get them on your side. We recommend severely penalizing any student who affiliates with a gang. But at the same time, schools should increase the rewards for youngsters who resist gang influence and use their leadership ability to advance the school's goals and objectives. School executives are sometimes too quick to go to war with a potential gang leader, and in doing so, they forget the value of coopting the adversary—an effective political strategy. Students who believe they're important to the school and who are doing useful things are less likely to find gangs appealing. It's good management, in other words, to identify leadership potential (especially among marginal students) and use it to the greater good of the school.

4. Don't close your doors at 3:15. To address the needs of marginal students who might be vulnerable to gangs, devise ways to keep students involved after regular school hours. All too often, these young people are on their own after school. Many of them come from single-parent families; their parents work long hours and don't have time to supervise or help coordinate after-school activities. What's more, these students often lack the talent to become members of the drama or debating club or the football team—and they aren't likely to volunteer for any activities you might provide. You'll have to seek these youngsters out and give them a highly structured program. For example, Rich East High School runs a daily 30-minute tutorial period, during which teachers must be in their rooms and no activities may begin.

5. Work with the police. Effective communication with law enforcement officials has several advantages. First, the local police department has a wealth of information and expertise about crime in the community. In addition, the police department can inform school personnel of the latest trends among local gangs and usually is willing to help school officials with in-service programs on gangs. Police officers also might be available to provide security and liaison services.

We have found that the presence of police officers serves as an excellent deterrent to gangs—especially if the officers work to develop positive relationships with marginal students, who are most vulnerable to problems of gang activity (see "We made police power a positive force in our schools," February 1989). We're convinced youngsters will feel greater conflict at the prospect of joining a gang if they have good relationships with local police officers.

6. Involve transfer students. Give new students activities and opportunities that will help them feel they belong. A well-designed program (which might include peer intervention) will help new youngsters acclimate—and help school officials identify student leaders and put their leadership to work in a positive direction.

7. Educate your teaching staff. Any effective staff development program must include a unit on the latest gang activity in your community. Ask law enforcement personnel to update teachers periodically with the latest information on gang symbols. Young people are not likely to flaunt gang symbols and other identifiers in the presence of knowledgeable teachers.

Gangs thrive on ignorance, and that means knowledge is the teacher's most important asset.

8. Get parents on your side. Parent support is critical to eliminating gang influence in the schools, but parent education is one of the most neglected areas of gang prevention. Parents have to learn to recognize the early signs of gang involvement, too, but so far, many schools have been reluctant to take responsibility for spreading the word. Providing parent education sessions is an excellent tactical move: Not only do such sessions help build alliances between school and community, but they help parents become more perceptive, especially during early stages of gang involvement. Also, parent education is an opportunity to coordinate an activity with law enforcement and local government to convey to parents a consistent message about gangs.

> All students need to see school as meaningful, especially those who are at risk of becoming involved in gangs.

A common problem school officials have with parents is their tendency to rationalize unacceptable behavior with the excuse that the kids are "just playing" or "will grow out of it." Such excuses can allow gang activity to thrive—and they can create a frustrating and potentially adversarial relationship between parents and schools. Addressing the issue of parent education only after serious problems have occurred is asking for trouble.

9. Find role models. Youngsters need more positive role models. Often, for example, educators and law enforcement personnel are the only authority figures many children see outside the home. In many suburban school systems, the number of minority teachers—especially males—is clearly inadequate. For example, black students make up about 11 percent of the secondary school population in Illinois, exclusive of Chicago. But only 4.3 percent of the teachers in this area are black. It's easy to rationalize this minority dearth by bemoaning the paucity of applicants. More productive is developing contacts and rapport with colleges of education and among current minority staff members.

10. Provide career counseling for marginal students. Reluctant learners are motivated only to the extent they see learning as meaningful—that is, relevant to their personal futures. All students need to see school as meaningful, especially those who are at risk of becoming involved in gangs. We recommend developing a career program with a specific goal of helping at-risk students find a meaningful connection between their current experiences at school and their futures. Young people who have acquired a sense of purpose and direction in their lives are much more likely to take school seriously—and much less likely to give in to gangs.

Media Violence

Between Censorship and License Is the Literate Consumer

by Wally Bowen

It's the question that won't go away: Does media violence promote real violence?

After all the evidence is cited, the debate about media violence quickly falls into a tired and frustrating pattern: either you are for government regulation of the media, or you support the First Amendment and are opposed to censorship.

This "either/or" choice shuts down discourse and diverts attention from what our experience tells us: that young people are impressionable, and that mass media help legitimize the belief that violence is the way the world works.

Given this impasse, we need a new way of talking about media violence. One approach begins by recognizing a little-known fact about commercial TV: When it comes to violent programming, censorship already exists.

> **Does media violence promote real violence?**

It's called "economic censorship." Here's how it works. Countless media texts—from cop shows to cartoons—depict violence as the preferred solution when conflicts arise. The violence formula is preferred because it's a tried-and-true way to grab and hold the attention of viewers, especially young viewers. Young viewers are the most prized audience for advertisers and their clients. They know that young people spend more freely and indiscriminately and have more years ahead of them as ardent consumers.

From *Education Week*, vol. 13, no. 25, p. 60, 47, March 16, 1994. Reprinted with permission.

Indeed, new TV networks—Fox and MTV—have been built on the fact that violent and sensational programming attracts and holds young viewers, especially in the age of "channel surfing."

Because it is formulaic, media violence is cheap and quick to produce. It doesn't require high-priced creative talent. Just as important, the visual language of media violence translates easily into foreign markets, where American-based media companies earn about half their revenue.

> ...violent and sensational programming attracts and holds young viewers, especially in the age of "channel surfing."

But here's the catch. In order to deliver viewers to commercial messages in a receptive mood, media violence must be neat and efficient. Advertisers do not want their products associated with the tragic consequences of violence. (Older viewers will recall that the social realism of "Playhouse 90" was unpalatable to advertisers, and thus the popular and critically acclaimed program was canceled.)

Commercial media divert attention from their economic censorship by portraying themselves as protectors of free speech. Their skill at using the First Amendment as a shield for profiteering will nullify any legislative attempts to regulate media violence. Even if a channel-blocking device—like the so-called V-chip—is mandated on new TV sets, only a small percentage of affluent and well-educated viewers are likely to buy and use it.

Moreover, the V-chip—as currently envisioned—would block only those programs designated by the industry as objectionable. Letting parents decide which programs to block would pose too great a threat to industry profits.

So while the current dance between Congress and the industry makes headlines, programming will change little, especially with the coming explosion of cable-TV channels. In the end, public antipathy toward commercial media will only increase. More disturbingly, however, we can also expect further erosion of public respect for the First Amendment.

There's got to be a better way. And there is. Unwittingly, apologists for commercial media point the way when they question how anyone can take media violence seriously. "It's make-believe. It's just entertainment," goes the industry refrain.

These apologists make such statements with a straight face because they make up a media elite which understands how media texts are constructed and how commercial forces shape programming. Media elites simply conform to the inevitable logic of the system. As the cultural historian Mark Crispin Miller has noted, "[T]he marketing imperative . . . resides in the very consciousness and day-to-day behavior of the media's general workforce."

Anyone who defies this logic by criticizing the products of commercial media "just doesn't get it." Media insiders simply assume the system's logic is self-evident.

But audiences do not think about TV as do the media-makers themselves, whose careers and hefty salaries are publicly on the line with each program or 30-second ad. "People don't really attend to TV," says Fred Baker, senior vice president of the McCann-Ericksen ad agency. "It's more of a subconscious or subliminal effect."

Says Lou Centilvre of the Foote Cone Belding agency: "People don't watch television like they're taking notes for an exam. They're half-conscious most of the time when they're watching television."

As a result, advertisers and programmers understand that their job is to "jolt the nerves of the half-attentive" with "stark pictures and a lightning pace," adds Mark Crispin Miller. Violence, whether it's the "Terminator" or the "Teenage Mutant Ninja Turtles," is an efficient tool for the job.

Stories built on the violence formula have more power and influence than their makers can afford to admit.

But stories built on the violence formula have more power and influence than their makers can afford to admit. Storytelling is how we organize society. Stories tell us who we are as a people, where we came from, and where we're going.

Especially powerful are stories about heroes. Before commercial mass media, heroic stories were grassroots creations tied to the needs and experience of local communities and cultures. With mass media, a historic change has occurred: Our culture's stories are increasingly manufactured by media insiders whose most important goal is to tell stories to mass audiences for the benefit of advertisers and their clients.

Young people are especially vulnerable in this new storytelling environment. Advertisers, no less than parents and teachers, understand that young people are walking bundles of needs and anxieties on the complex path to adulthood. Stories about heroes have always been important maps for that journey, because heroes exude power and a strong sense of self, just what young people are seeking.

By understanding the profit motives behind media violence, young people are less likely to let violence define their view of reality.

Today's stories, however, serve the interests of the few at the expense of the many. This truism was foreshadowed years ago with L. Frank Baum's early critique of media pyrotechnics: The moment when Toto pulls back the curtain to reveal the real Wizard of Oz.

Media elites have seen behind the curtain. They know how the pseudo-realities of TV and movies are constructed. We need to give our young people this insider's knowledge. Fortunately, there's a way to do this. It's called media literacy.

Media literacy takes students behind the scenes to show how special effects, editing, camera angles, sound, and lighting are used to create powerful illusions of reality. Media literacy also delves into the economics of media and examines how the needs of advertisers dictate what we're offered by commercial media.

For example, media literacy pulls the curtain back on what advertisers and marketing experts routinely discuss in their trade publications: that toymakers make more money off boys, and that boys most often determine which channel is watched on Saturday morning. That's why cartoons are dominated by male action heroes who use violence to resolve conflict.

Media literacy also reveals how different audiences respond to media. For example, during the Persian Gulf War, researchers at the University of Massachusetts found that heavy TV viewers were more likely to support the war and to mistake Kuwait for a democracy.

Similarly, the media researcher George Gerbner finds that

heavy TV viewers are more likely to believe they live in a "mean world." Used in the classroom, this insight can lead students to pose interesting questions: How does the "mean world" outlook influence the political and social behavior of heavy TV viewers? Are heavy TV viewers more likely to own guns? Are they more likely to use them?

These are just a couple of examples of how media literacy helps students think critically about the media world we live in. By understanding the profit motives behind media violence, young people are less likely to let violence define their view of reality. When industry apologists argue that TV and movies simply hold a mirror up to reality, media-literate young people know it's not that simple.

Fortunately, media literacy is not just another add-on to our schools' already overloaded curriculum. Media literacy enlivens how our schools teach critical thinking by serving as a bridge between the classroom and the world in which our young people live most of their waking lives. Indeed, the school curricula in many states such as North Carolina and New Mexico have numerous references to thinking critically about mass media.

The missing link, however, is teacher training. While media-literacy training has been conducted in Canada, Australia, and Britain for more than two decades, only North Carolina, New Mexico, and Massachusetts have begun offering media-literacy training for teachers. We must do more. Media literacy must be put on the fast track in our schools, communities, and teacher training programs.

Media literacy protects our tradition of free speech by side-stepping the First Amendment shield used by commercial media to protect their profits. Media literacy is not a cure-all for violence, but it should be part of any comprehensive effort to address the problem. It's our only real tool for reining in a media culture that is out of control.

Effects of Violence

by Stephanie Kadel and Joseph Follman

E ducators witness every day the many effects of violence in their schools. This subsection discusses the emotional and behavioral effects that violence has on the lives of students and teachers as well as the legal ramifications of violence for schools.

ON STUDENTS

Not only does a school's environment affect learning, but more than any other setting it influences how students—especially high school students—conform to society. School's internal life influences how all students behave, often more powerfully than the home or community. It is un-likely that a student immersed in a school environment of delinquency will form a more responsible view of society at large. J.A. Rapp, F. Carrington, and G. Nicholson, *School Crime and Violence: Victims' Rights,* 1992

> **If one student uses a gun to settle an altercation, others will feel they need guns too.**

Students are affected by violence in a number of ways. The most obvious is the physical harm that can result. For example, when more weapons—especially guns—are brought into school, common student conflicts such as arguments over girl-friends or boyfriends, disputes about possessions, and name calling can become fatal interactions. If one student uses a gun to settle an altercation, others will feel they need guns too. As Gaustad (1991) concludes, "a cycle of fear begins, prompting an

From *Hot Topics: Usable Research, Reducing School Violence,* the SouthEastern Regional Vision for Education, 1993, p. 61–64. Reprinted with permission.

escalation in an arms race where youths seek ever more powerful forms of 'protection'" (p. 7).

Fear in school is another serious and pervasive result, and fear leads to other effects as well. As early as 1976, a Dade County, Florida, survey revealed that one-fifth of the respondents in secondary schools reported that their ability to learn in class was hampered by their fear of other students (Dade County Public Schools, 1976). A more recent study showed that eight percent of students skipped one day of school a month because they feared for their safety (Learning Publications, 1988).

The five top school policies that junior high and high school students say lead to misconduct:
1. Closed campuses
2. Teachers can smoke but not students
3. Not enough time between classes
4. Dress codes
5. "Dressing out" requirements for physical education
                    Task Force on School Discipline, 1990

Wayne and Rubel (1982) point out other effects of student fear: Apprehensiveness among students has an obvious impact on the business of education: it reduces concentration on assigned tasks, creates an atmosphere of mistrust, and undermines school morale. More subtly, the school administrator's inability to reduce fear directly tells students that staff are not in control of the school's social climate—that student disorder is more powerful than the adult call for order (pp. 230-231).

Research also suggests that students who feel afraid in school are often those who end up committing acts of violence. Aggressive students who are placed in a secure and contained environment are likely to demonstrate more internal control over their own actions. Left in an unsafe environment, they develop a mistrust of adults, experience increased feelings of fear, and demonstrate inappropriate behaviors that become harder and harder to modify (Ditter, 1988).

Fear is not the only psychological effect of violence on children and youth, however. Many children who are exposed to violence suffer post-traumatic stress syndrome similar to that experienced by combat soldiers. A study conducted by the University of Alabama at Birmingham revealed that 43 percent of a sample of inner-city youth aged 7 to 19 had witnessed a homicide. Researchers discovered an emerging epidemic of post-traumatic stress syndrome that included symptoms such as nightmares, difficulty with concentration at school, guilt over one's own survival, lack of interest in fun activities, and feelings of distance from parents and friends (Morganthau et al., 1992; NSSC, 1990a).

> ...students who feel afraid in school are often those who end up committing acts of violence.

Violence in the school and community can also prevent students from taking advantage of after-school educational, recreational, and employment opportunities which can be of immense value for their personal development. According to Wetzel (1988), "The hundreds of thousands of attempted or completed violent crimes have a powerful influence on everyday decisions. Many youths and their parents are persuaded that it is not safe for young people to attend night school, participate in after-school activities, or work at a job that requires late hours" (p. 5).

ON TEACHERS

In addition to the risk of physical harm resulting from school violence, teachers too can suffer emotional effects. Studies reveal that teachers who have witnessed violent incidents, fear violence, or cope daily with disruptive students often exhibit symptoms of stress akin to those of combat soldiers. They can suffer from fatigue, headaches, stomach pains, and hypertension (Gaustad, 1991). Because teachers are given limited training on how to deal with violent students in their classrooms, trying to maintain order and teach class at the same time often leads to stress and feelings of ineffectiveness that fuel teacher burnout and high attrition rates (McKelvey, 1988). Some teachers even fall into the same trap as students and bring weapons to school to protect themselves.

A survey conducted by the National Center for Education Statistics (1991) found that 48 percent of the teachers in the sample reported that a lack of or inadequate alternative programs for disruptive students limited their ability to maintain discipline in their classrooms; 34 percent stated that disruptive behavior interfered with their teaching. These two issues had more of an effect on teaching and discipline than any other factors, including student drug and alcohol use, lack of support from administration, or inadequate school security personnel.

LITIGATION

Schools are often charged with negligence when students are injured or traumatized, and the courts have held that "although a school may not be expected to be a guarantor or insurer of the safety of its students, it is expected to provide, in addition to an intellectual climate, a physical environment harmonious with the purposes of an educational institution" (Rapp et al., 1992, p. 17). In general, however, schools are not usually held liable unless the violence was reasonably foreseeable.

> Many children and teachers who are exposed to violence suffer post-traumatic stress syndrome similar to that experienced by combat soldiers.

Does the U.S Constitution impose a responsibility on schools and districts to protect students? The Supreme Court has never ruled on this issue, but most lower courts have found that schools do not have a "custodial" relationship akin to, for example, that between administrators and patients at a state mental hospital, even though students are compelled to attend school (Walsh, 1992, p. 10). A recent circuit court case in Texas, however, reached a different conclusion. It ruled that compulsory attendance laws give schools "functional custody" of students during the school hours and that it is a reasonable expectation "that the state will provide a safe school environment." Appealed to the Supreme Court, this case raises concerns for school officials that they may be deemed responsible for violence that is less directly connected to schools, such as gang violence or attacks on the school's neighborhood (Walsh, 1992).

In 1992, the high court ruled that in cases of sexual abuse, school officials who are aware of the problem but fail to take appropriate action to stop it may be held liable and sued for monetary damages (Lumsden, 1992). Schools have also been held liable when instances of negligent hiring, training, and supervision of sexually abusive teachers has led to sexual abuse of students or when improper supervision of students or inadequate security has permitted sexually abusive behavior. Adoption of a strong policy prohibiting sexual harassment provides some assurance that prevention is a priority and that complaints will be investigated thoroughly. A sample policy statement published by the Florida Department of Education, *Guidelines for Policies Addressing Sexual Misconduct Toward Students in Public Schools* (1992), addresses this issue. See the Annotated Resources section for further information.

California has approved a state constitutional right to safe schools as part of its Victim's Bill of Rights. This amendment guarantees all K-12 students the inalienable right to attend campuses which are "safe, secure and peaceful" (Sawyer, 1988) and gives citizens the right take legal action to ensure that they are. Rapp et al. (1992) state that a school "has a duty to guard its students against dangers of which it has actual knowledge and those which it should reasonably anticipate" (p. 74), and recommend that schools work to assure that students and staff are protected from the following risks:

- foreseeable criminal activity,
- student crime or violence that can be prevented by adequate supervision,
- identifiably dangerous students,
- dangerous individuals negligently admitted to school,
- dangerous individuals negligently placed in school, and
- school administrators, teachers, and staff who have been negligently selected, retained, or trained (p. 18).

REFERENCES

Dade County Public Schools. (1976). *Experience of teachers and students with disruptive behavior in the Dade public schools.* Miami, FL: Office of Alternative Education.

Ditter, B. (1988, Winter). Emotional safety and growing up. *School Safety,* 12–15.

Florida Department of Education. (1992). *1991 Florida youth risk behavior survey report.* Tallahassee, FL: Prevention Center.

Gaustad, J. (1991). Schools respond to gangs and violence [Special issue]. *Oregon School Study Council (OSSC) Bulletin, 34*(9).

Learning Publications. (1988). Shocking violence in schools. *School Intervention Report , 7*(1), 1–2.

Lumsden, L.S. (1992, December). Combating sexual harassment. *ERIC Digest, Number 75.*

McKelvey, C.A. (1988). Children who kill. *School Safety, Spring,* 12–16.

Morganthau, T., Annin, P., McCormick, J., Wingert, P., Foote, D., Manly, H., & King, P. (1992. March 9). It's not just New York...Big cities, small towns: More and more guns in younger and younger hands. *Newsweek,* 25–26, 29.

National Center for Education Statistics. (1991). *Teacher survey on safe, disciplined, and drug-free schools.* Washington, DC: U.S. Department of Education, Office of Educational Research and Improvement.

Rapp, J. A., Carrrington, F., & Nicholson, G. (1992). *School crime and violence: Victim's rights.* Malibu, CA: National School Safety Center.

Sawyer, K. A. (1988). *The right to safe schools: A newly recognized inalienable right.* Malibu, CA: National School Safety Center.

Task Force on School Discipline. (1990). *Report of the Task Force on School Discipline.* Tallahassee: Florida Department of Education.

Walsh, M. (1992, December 2). Suits spurring courts to rethink schools' liability to protect students from harm. *Education Week, 12*(13), 1, 10.

Wayne, I., & Rubel, R. J. (1982). Student fear in secondary schools. *The Urban Review, 14*(3), 197–237.

Wetzel, J. R. (1988, Spring). Kids and crime. *School Safety,* 4–7.

Prevention: People, Policies, and Programs

Section Two's articles discuss the need for establishing a safe environment and how teachers can create positive classroom climates that help prevent violence from occurring or escalating. The roles of educational professionals, parents, pupils, and the community in combating the problem are discussed. It is clear that violence cannot be addressed solely by the schools. The problem requires the effort and attention of the entire community.

The article by Stephanie Kadel and Joseph Follman from the SouthEastern Regional Vision for Education touches on methods for preventing school violence. Methods include involving the principal, enhancing campus safety, improving teaching techniques, and involving parents and the community.

Mary Lynn Cantrell provides a comprehensive picture of how to deal with gangs, while Walt Landen and Pat Ordovensky give insight into what other administrators can and have been doing to combat the violence.

The articles by Debra L. Williams, Richard F. Arthur, and Susan E. Craig make suggestions for activities and programs that can be implemented within the school setting. These articles offer techniques and responses to attacks that may otherwise lead to anger and violence.

Marc Posner investigates current school-based violence prevention programs. He shows that most are too simplistic and have experienced little success.

The overriding message in all of these articles is that teaching students to care about themselves and others is the first step in creating a school environment that fosters understanding and tolerance for differences.

Strategies to Prevent School Violence

by Stephanie Kadel and Joseph Follman

While knowing how to handle violent incidents in school is important, preventing violence is clearly a better strategy. To be most effective, violence prevention requires a unified, holistic approach to strategic planning. Not only should the school safety committee address current problems, but it should also develop long-term strategies designed to deter future acts of violence. Since the level of violence varies from school to school, having an individual school plan is vital. Even schools and districts with limited resources can have effective prevention programs as long as the strategies they design are complementary [complimentary] and directed toward clearly identified goals (CDC, 1992).

> To be most effective, violence prevention requires a unified, holistic approach to strategic planning.

1. CREATING A SAFE SCHOOL ENVIRONMENT

The first step in creating a safe school environment is analyzing existing incidents of violence to ensure that the members of the school safety committee understand the scope of the problem. To this end, the committee can review incident reports to identify what kinds of crimes are committed, who commits them, and where the crimes are committed. The committee can also gather useful material from truancy and attendance records; attitude surveys; and informal interviews with students,

From *Hot Topics: Usable Research, Reducing School Violence*, the SouthEastern Regional Vision for Education, 1993, p. 21–47. Reprinted with permission.

faculty, staff, parents, and community members (California State DOE, 1989). With this information in hand, the safety committee can seek answers to the following types of questions:

• How is school violence perceived by the students, teachers, parents, school security, school and district administrators, and police?

• How are criminal acts committed at the school handled? Are existing discipline procedures applied? Are all or selected incidents reported to the police? Are parents informed? Are juvenile authorities involved?

• How do police respond to school crime (Blount, 1986)?

District officials should stress to school administrators that problems with violence are not indicative of poor leadership. To encourage principals to acknowledge the existence of a problem, district officials should respond with suggestions and assistance rather than recriminations (Gaustad, 1991). An assessment that provides a clear picture of the current situation can serve as the foundation for long-term prevention efforts. States or large districts can help by forming "safety check teams" that will visit schools and request help; review discipline policies, building security, and prevention strategies; and offer recommendations and financial and technical assistance for improvements. Examination of a wide range of successful school violence reduction programs suggests that there are a number of components involved in creating a safe school environment, including school climate, the role of the principal, enhancing campus safety, a safe school building, the school's code of conduct, student involvement, staff development, and peer interaction.

> If students, parents, and staff feel a sense of community and ownership in the school, they are more likely to work with each other rather than against each other.

School Climate

A positive school climate is key to preventing violence. If students, parents, and staff feel a sense of community and ownership in the school, they are more likely to work with each other rather than against each other. If a school has a climate in which staff, students, and parents feel safe and welcome, victims of a violence incident may find the healing process easier as the school reestablishes its supportive and secure atmosphere.

The physical climate is also important. According to a report from the U.S. Department of Education (1988), the more the school looks like a workshop, a library, a restaurant, or a conference center and less like a prison or institution, the more conducive the environment is to learning. While most principals are aware of the benefits of having a positive school climate, it is useful for a school safety committee or school improvement team to examine efforts to improve the school climate to determine if those efforts include addressing the specific issue of violence.

The Role of the Principal

The role of the principal is critical in the development of a positive school climate and a safe school. Principals who have succeeded in creating safe and peaceful schools out of violence-ridden campuses emphasize the importance of maintaining a high profile as well as individual and group contacts with students (Greenbaum, Turner, & Stephens, 1989). In addition to walking the halls and school grounds regularly (a considerable deterrent to crime and violence), these principals frequently visit classrooms and always make themselves available to teachers, students, and parents who wish to meet with them. They keep in touch with formal and informal student leaders to get their perspectives on school events and to enlist their support in involving more students in school activities. Ciminillo (1980) stresses that principals "must express sincere feelings toward students, a genuine interest in their lives, and a real belief that they have the potential to become successful adults" (p. 87).

Enhancing Campus Safety

Many attempts to make schools safe are more reactive than proactive. Initiatives such as installing metal detectors, hiring armed guards, or searching students' belongings must be used with caution. Effective administrators avoid inadvertently instilling more fear and mistrust in students by implementing policies that are excessively oppressive or demeaning or that risk violating students' rights. As Gaustad (1991) cautions, "Even the best deterrence efforts can't totally eliminate the possibility of violence, and putting too much emphasis on security may frighten children unnecessarily" (p. 36).

In some situations, however, establishing order may require stronger-than-usual deterrents and controls such as the use of police officers or metal detectors. If violence at a school is serious enough to warrant such tactics, they must (1) be tailored to meet the problem at hand, (2) employ easy-to-understand procedures, and (3) be clearly explained to all. In addition, plans should be made for gradually reducing or phasing them out as other, more positive measures—such as improving the school climate and educating students to be nonviolent—take effect. School officials will need to remember that the cost of providing extraordinary security measures subtracts from the overall budget for improvements in curriculum, staff development, and instructional materials that are necessary for an improved education (Ciminillo, 1980). Table 6 describes a number of strategies for reducing school violence and increasing school safety. The strategies are divided into categories depending on their primary purposes.

> Even the best deterrence efforts can't totally eliminate the possibility of violence, and putting too much emphasis on security may frighten children unnecessarily.

Table 6
Strategies that Help Reduce Violence in School
Increasing Surveillance and Supervision Around the School

- Assign school staff to patrol problem areas such as hallways, stairwells, locker rooms, bathrooms, cafeterias, and school grounds.
- Enlist the help of parents or other volunteers to monitor the front entrance or patrol the halls. (This strategy is not recommended if violence is common and volunteers are likely to be harmed.)
- Train parents, students, or other volunteers to be hall monitors. As monitors, these volunteers would not have the same authority as police/security officers, but they can be prepared to intervene in fights and defuse other violent situations better than untrained

volunteers. Volunteers are, of course, significantly less expensive than security officers.

- If safety is a concern before and after school, designate a safe, centralized location for students and staff to gather. Ask teachers who work late to work in pairs or teams in the designated area.

- In neighborhoods where students are afraid to walk to and from school, map out the safest routes and escort students as needed. Encourage students to walk in groups, and ask police to patrol the routes that students use during the morning and afternoon.

- Hire security officers to patrol the school, check student identification, and be present at athletic events and other school activities. Officers may be "leased" from local police forces, although this approach can be expensive and gives the school less control over the officers' duties. Some large school districts have their own police force trained to work with students and hired to handle school crime. Another option is to contract with a security company, which is often more affordable but can result in poorly trained officers with a high turnover rate. Schools should implement the least obtrusive security policies necessary. If these officers are to be viewed as potential confidants for students—not just as deterrents to crime—they should be accessible to students. They should also be provided training in working and talking with young people and in the cultural backgrounds of the students. (Gaustad, 1991; NSSC, 1990b)

Keeping Weapons out of School
- Announce and post the school's policy against weapons possession and the consequences for bringing weapons to school.
- Clearly define what constitutes a weapon.
- Limit or prohibit student access to cars during the school day.
- Define lockers as equipment of the school district which students are allowed to use temporarily for convenience; specify that lockers are not private storage spaces. Post signs in the halls that clearly state that, if administrators are given reasonable suspicion, lockers can and will be searched. Notify students if their lockers will be searched, and allow individual students to be present.
- Use metal detectors to check students for weapons as they enter school. Although a quarter of the nation's large urban school districts now use metal detectors to search students for weapons, metal detectors have significant disadvantages: they are expensive, may give the impression that students are being treated like convicts, and are not as effective as they might seem because students can still pass weapons through school windows or hide them outside and pick them up later in the day. Metal detectors are also im-

practical for schools with many entrances and with several buildings connected by outdoor walkways. A compromise may be to periodically require students who have been suspended for weapons
possession to pass through a metal detector.
- Refer all weapons offenders for counseling. (CDC, 1992; Dade
County Public Schools, 1988; Grant, 1992; Morganthau et al., 1992;
NSSC, 1990a, 1990b; Prophet, 1990)

Keeping Unauthorized Persons Off Campus
- Limit and supervise the entry and movement of persons on school
grounds; monitor delivery and loading entrances as well as main
doors.
- Provide a list of visitor regulations to students, parents, and community members and post it at all entrances.
- Require visitors to sign in a the main office and wear identification
badges while at the school.
- Use I.D. cards or another identification system for students.
- Designate one entrance for visitors during the school day and en-
force this policy at all other entrances.
- Install emergency alarms on rarely-used doors to discourage their
use.
- Register all staff and student cars with the school and require park-
ing stickers for legal parking on school grounds.
- Keep a record of all cars that enter school parking lots illegally.
Note the make, style, color, and license plate number as well as the
date seen. Refer to this record in case of theft, vandalism, or intrusive behavior.
- Establish a closed campus policy and require all who enter or leave
the school (during the day) to sign in and out.
- Question anyone loitering outside the school.
- Station security/police officers at athletic and school-sponsored
events. Announce to students in advance the behavior that will be
expected of them.
- Seek a formal agreement from gang members that school will be
neutral territory. Prohibit all gang-related activities and traits—
such as special clothing, hairstyles, colors, insignias, and hand ges-
tures—in school and at school-sponsored events. Be especially
wary of non-student gang members loitering around school
campuses.
- If an unauthorized person is determined to be a student from another school, notify the student's home school and ask that the
student's parents be notified. (Dade County Public Schools, 1988;
Gaustad, 1991; NSSC, 1990a; Speck, 1992)

Enlisting Support for Preventing Violence
- Invite parents and students to contribute ideas about school safety in a suggestion box. Respond to all comments and thank personally those who make useful recommendations. Such a container can also serve as a "nomination box" for recognizing employees or students who have made a significant contribution to school safety efforts.
- Hold group forums to encourage students and/or parents to express opinions and concerns about the school's safety and to ask questions about school policies.
- Devise a school reporting system to enable students, staff, and parents to report violent behavior or suspected trouble anonymously. Offer rewards.
- Suggest that students avoid wearing valuable clothing, shoes, and jewelry to schools where thefts are likely.
- Have teachers, administrators, counselors, and others meet regularly as a team to discuss problems of disruptive students and plan individual strategies to help them before they become violent.
- Ask school psychologists, counselors, and/or teachers to visit the homes of disruptive and potentially violent students.
- Act on rumors; talk to students who are rumored to be having behavioral or social problems with others and take seriously student reports of possible fights.
- Encourage bus drivers and custodians, who are good sources of information about scheduled fights or weapons brought to campus, to report such information routinely. (Blauvelt, 1981; California State DOE, 1989; Greenbaum, Gonzalez, & Ackley, 1989; May, 1992; NSSC, 1990a; Perry & Duke, 1978; Prophet, 1990; Rapp et al., 1992)

Using Other Prevention Strategies
- Remove graffiti as soon as it is discovered.
- Offer school- or community-based activities for students after school and on the weekends. Institute after-school academic and recreational programs for latchkey students.
- Conduct a thorough background check on anyone applying to work in the school to assure that no one is hired who has been convicted of sexual assault, child molestation, or pornography or has a history of violent criminal behavior. Do not make hiring decisions before the check is completed. (California State DOE, 1989; CDC, 1992; Gaustad, 1991; May, 1992; NSSC, 1989, 1990a; Perry & Duke, 1978; Prophet, 1990; Rapp et al., 1992)

A Safe School Building

When new schools are built, architects, educators, and security experts should work together to design the safest yet most appealing school building possible. For maximum visibility, one school superintendent recommends building schools as "wheels," with the main office at the hub and halls forming the spokes. Schools might also be located where they are visible from homes and businesses, with all entries and administrative offices visible from bordering streets (NSSC, 1990a). Table 7 offers a number of suggestions for improving the safety of existing school buildings. For more complete information on security systems, building designs, and "target hardening" tactics, see the National School Safety Center's *School Safety Check Book* (1990b).

Table 7
Creating a Safe School Building

- Light all hallways adequately during the day.
- Close off unused stairwells or do not leave areas of school unused.
- Install all lockers in areas where they are easily visible.
- Minimize blind spots or use convex mirrors to allow hall monitors to see around corners.
- Prohibit posters in classroom windows.
- Install an alarm system and/or a closed-circuit television monitoring system.
- Keep buildings clean and maintained.
- Locate playground equipment where it is easily observed.
- Limit roof access by keeping dumpsters away from building walls.
- Cover drainpipes so they cannot be scaled.
- Avoid decorative ledges; plant trees at least ten feet from buildings.
- Trim trees and shrubs to limit outside hiding places for people or weapons.
- Keep school grounds free of gravel or loose rock surfaces.
- Ensure vehicle access around the building(s) for night surveillance and emergency vehicles.
- Design parking lots to discourage through traffic; install speed bumps.
- Mix faculty and student parking.
- Create a separate parking lot for students and staff who arrive early or stay late, and monitor these lots carefully.

- Use fencing and gates with discretion and choose attractive wrought iron styles instead of chain link fences. Secure them with heavy-duty padlocks.
- Establish a policy to have the school campus fully lighted or totally dark at night. (Total darkness has been shown to reduce theft and vandalism while conserving energy.)
- Keep a complete list of staff members who have keys to the building(s).

(California State DOE, 1989; CDC, 1992; NSSC, 1990a, 1990b; Speck, 1992)

The School's Code of Conduct

A discipline code should clearly identify school rules and acceptable student behaviors. As Greenbaum, Turner, and Stephens (1989) point out, "We tend to get not only what we expect, what we deserve, and what we measure, but also, perhaps most importantly, what we 'put up with.' The three F's of good school administration include being firm, friendly and fair—in that order" (p. 59). The best discipline code is short and easy to understand with clearly stated consequences for actions (NSSC, 1990b). Successful codes of conduct are written with student input and clearly define the roles, rights, and responsibilities of all persons involved in the school. According to Gottfredson (1983), the code should include only rules that will be enforced: "If the code violation is not worth disciplining, it is not worth being in the code in the first place. Undisciplined violations breed disrespect and noncompliance" (p. 191). Research on school violence emphasizes the necessity of enforcing discipline codes consistently and fairly (California State DOE, 1989; Gaustad, 1991; NSSC, 1990b; U. S. Department of Justice, 1986). Administrators should, therefore, avoid punishing students as "examples" and discipline all students in the same way for the same behavior.

> The discipline code is not only a set of rules for students to follow, it also informs teachers, parents, and others exactly what kind of behavior is expected of students at a particular school.

The discipline code is not only a set of rules for students to follow; it also informs teachers, parents, and others exactly what kind of behavior is expected of students at a particular school. A copy of the school discipline code should be sent to parents at the start of every school year and distributed to students and staff (Greenbaum, Turner, & Stephens, 1989). The discipline code should be reviewed periodically and updated to reflect changes in the school and surrounding environment. It is important for schools to use standard definitions for code violations so that everyone will understand what specific terms and infractions entail.

Successful codes of conduct are written with student input and clearly define the roles, rights, and responsibilities of all persons involved in the school.

Communicating the Code of Conduct

Teachers should be encouraged to discuss the code of conduct with their students, make sure everyone understands its purpose and expectations, and seek agreement from students to follow it. Many schools designate homeroom or a certain class taken by all students, such as English, as the setting for making students aware of policies. This is more effective than trying to tell the entire school at once in an assembly or over the intercom because it allows for discussion in a less formal setting.

In addition to explaining the rules of student behavior, codes of conduct should

• clearly define the roles, rights, and responsibilities of all persons involved in the school setting including students, teachers, administrators and support staff, as well as parents, and police;

• provide a procedure for student appeals;

• provide a system of rewards for positive behavior; and

• describe the sequence(s) of consequences for misbehavior (Governor's Task Force on School Violence and Vandalism, 1979, pp. 13-14).

Regarding violent behavior, the National School Safety Center (1990a) recommends that the discipline code clearly state that anyone who is "guilty of assault, violent crime or weapon possession on campus will be arrested, and the school will vigorously assist in prosecuting the offender" (p. 130). Greenbaum, Turner, and Stephens (1989) also recommend that the following rules be included in a school discipline code:

• Striking another person may be considered a criminal act and may be dealt with as such.

• Every student has a right to be secure and safe from threats and harassment.

• Anyone bringing weapons onto school grounds will be considered armed and dangerous, and the police will be called.

> **Students have a right and a duty to be involved in the prevention and reduction of school violence.**

• Crimes against property and any other violations of the law will be treated as such (p. 60).

In addition, a discipline code should also include policy against

• bigotry,
• hate crimes,
• sexual harassment, and
• sexual assault.

The policies should explain what kinds of actions will be deemed as violations and provide for appropriate sanctions (Bodinger-DeUriarte & Sancho, 1992). When writing the discipline code, administrators need to decide how they will distinguish between criminal and non-criminal acts and what actions will be taken (U. S. Department of Justice, 1986). Gaustad (1991) reminds administrators that many of the altercations that take place in school, such as bullying, threats, intimidation, and fights in which one student is the victim are indeed crimes. Consistent rule enforcement will require administrators to always deal with these activities using the same set of standards.

Student Involvement

Students have a duty and a right to be involved in the prevention and reduction of school violence. They also have a responsibility to avoid becoming victims to the extent they are able by, for example, walking in groups and avoiding high-risk areas of campus (Rapp et al., 1992). To ensure student involvement, schools should encourage all students to participate in decisions about school safety and discipline procedures and see that student leaders are trained to represent their fellow students on these issues (Scrimger & Elder, 1981).

Table 8
Strategies to Increase Student Involvement
in Violence Prevention Efforts

- Create a group of student leaders, representing formal and informal groups, to promote student responsibility for a safe school environment.
- Involve students in decision making about school rules; the discipline code, curriculum, books and materials; evaluations of teachers and administrators; and the development of after-school recreational, tutoring, and mentoring programs.
- Encourage teachers to involve students in decision making at the classroom level.
- Encourage students to establish local chapters of national safety groups, such as SADD (Students Against Drunk Driving) and Youth Crime Watch.
- Establish a crime prevention club, similar to a neighborhood watch for the school, which involves reporting incidents and offering rewards.
- Teach students to be responsible for their own safety and emphasize the importance of reporting suspicious activities or people on campus. Most administrators in urban school districts find out about a weapon in the school through a student tip.
- Teach courses in personal safety and assertiveness.
- Train students to use conflict-resolution techniques and act as student mediators for conflicts among their peers.
- Use students to teach their peers about violence prevention. A similar strategy has been used successfully to teach adolescents about avoiding alcohol, cigarette, and drug use.
- Involve students in community service projects to improve the school and community environment and to help them learn personal responsibility.

(CDC, 1992; Gaustad, 1991; Governor's Task Force, 1979; Greenbaum, Gonzalez, & Ackley, 1989; NSSC, 1989, 1990a; Perry & Duke, 1978)

Peer Interaction

Students may benefit from long-term behavior modification techniques such as peer mentoring, peer mediation, guided group discussions, or behavior contracts (Governor's Task Force, 1979). Such programs give students a safe and controlled outlet in which they can speak with their peers about their problems and develop solutions. Students are empowered to make decisions about what the consequences of their acts should be.

In peer mediation, students are trained to help other students resolve conflicts. The peer mediators encourage disputants to use nonviolent ways of resolving differences and to arrive at mutually satisfactory solutions. For many students, being able to sit down and talk about disputes without the threat or fear of violence is an entirely new experience (Florida DOE, 1992).

> **The peer mediators encourage disputants to use nonviolent ways of resolving differences and to arrive at mutually satisfactory solutions.**

Ideally representative of the entire student body, peer mediators are also trained in conflict management and communication skills to enable them to defuse anger, conflicts, rumors, and tension among peers (NSSC, 1990b). This training typically includes discussions of possible responses to and consequences of violence as well as role playing of mediated conflicts (CDC, 1992).

An elementary principal whose school has instituted peer mediation notes these benefits to students:

• Conflict managers learn and reinforce "people skills" that will be useful throughout their lives.

• Conflict-prone students, after repeatedly being guided through the resolution process, learn that they can find peaceful alternatives to conflict and that both sides in a dispute can "win."

• All students who observe the process, even if they are not directly involved as mediators or disputants, learn some of the skills (Welch, 1989, pp. 23, 31).

Another peer-directed strategy is student court (or peer review, honor court, or peer court), in which students have the authority to make disciplinary decisions about fellow students. Selected by their peers or teachers, these student judges, lawyers and jurors are trained by local justice system experts to try cases, make real judgments, and pass real sentences (Greenbaum, Gonzalez, & Ackley, 1989). Students on the court have full knowledge of the school's code of conduct and are trained to be consistent and non-judgmental in their actions. In most schools with student courts, offenders have the option of being tried by the student court or accepting standard administrative discipline procedures (Scrimger & Elder, 1981).

Staff Development and Inservice

Just as any school improvement effort requires staff development, efforts to improve a school's safety must address the informational and hands-on training needs of teachers and other school staff. Staff safety workshops might emphasize the relationship between a safe school and a quality education as well as the need for public support of the school and the importance of safety to garnering that support (Greenbaum, Gonzalez, & Ackley, 1989). Such workshops would also include information about proposed violence prevention strategies and the specific responsibilities of school staff for maintaining a safe environment.

Staff development in violence prevention may be provided by a variety of community resources (many of them available at no or little cost) including police officers, lawyers, judges, health and human service providers, probation officers, and representatives from institutions for juvenile offenders (Greenbaum, Gonzalez, & Ackley, 1989). Seminars and workshops can be videotaped for future reference and for new employees (California State DOE, 1989). Table 9 suggests topics for staff development seminars which can be offered as part of the school's comprehensive violence reduction plan.

In addition to seminars and workshops, school staff can learn about many of these issues by observing colleagues and other professionals at work and sharing among themselves (Governor's Task Force, 1979). Universities and colleges should also be encouraged to include topics in personal and school safety in their courses for education majors, teachers, administrators, and counselors (California State DOE, 1989).

2. TEACHING NONVIOLENCE AND ALTERNATIVES TO VIOLENCE

Violence and empathy are mutually exclusive.
J. Gaustad, *Schools Respond to Gangs and Violence,* 1991

While a school can do much to create a safer environment for its students, preventing violence is the best long-term strategy. An effective way to prevent school violence is to teach students the behaviors, skills, and values that are associated with peaceful behavior within the school as well as the larger community. This section identifies a variety of instructional strategies designed to promote school safety by teaching students how to avoid conflict or resolve it peacefully. Table 10 lists a number of educational ideas to help prevent violence.

> An effective way to prevent school violence is to teach students the behaviors, skills, and values that are associated with peaceful behavior.

Table 10
Educational Strategies for Violence Prevention

- Teach students about the nature and extent of violence in society and in their community. This is especially important for young people who have a natural tendency to believe they are immortal and to adopt an "it can't happen to me" attitude. Complement discussions of violence with instruction on how to avoid becoming a victim of crime.
- Prevent hate crimes by discussing and rejecting stereotypes of minority groups, encouraging interaction with members of different cultures, and encouraging an appreciation of diversity. Also, ensure that educational materials reflect the many cultures of this society.
- Use existing courses to teach safety topics. For example, social studies or current events classes can discuss social unrest and resulting violence in society, English classes can write essays on self-esteem or interpersonal conflict, and art classes can design anti-violence posters.
- Teach students about the damaging effects of sexual harassment and sexual assault. From an early age, children can learn the difference between "good touching" and "bad touching," and that "no

means no." Older students can have group discussions about dating and relationship expectations.

- Instruct students in laws that affect juveniles and the consequences for breaking these laws. Take students to visit a jail. Says Kean (1981), "The opportunity to observe incarceration firsthand and to discuss with prisoners their lives, purportedly has the impact of shock therapy" (p. 12). Encourage respect for the law through discussions of social contract theory and other purposes for creating laws.
- Tell students about the lethal impact of guns and the legal implications of carrying or using a gun. Try to counteract the attractiveness of guns to young people. While emphasizing that students should not carry guns, discuss gun safety as well.
- Videotape television news stories that describe actual incidents involving guns and have students watch and discuss them.
- Teach both elementary and secondary students to avoid gang activities and provide them with alternative programs to meet their social and recreational needs. Invite guest speakers who work with gang members, such as law enforcement or probation officers, to speak to classes or assemblies. Former gang members who have "turned their lives around" may also tell stories that inspire students to keep away from gangs.
- Teach problem-solving skills in both academic and social settings.
- Tell students that anger is an acceptable feeling, but that acting on anger in violent ways is unacceptable. Teach children how to express their anger nonviolently or to confront the source of the anger with plans to "work it out" through peaceful, problem-solving discussions.
- Offer assistance in finding jobs, especially to students who are at risk of dealing drugs or joining a gang because they feel they have no legitimate way to make a living and take care of themselves.
- Teach students social skills such as how to use self-control, communicate well with others, form and maintain friendships, etc.
- Talk with students about being "good sports" to discourage the disruptive and sometimes violent behavior that can break out at school athletic events. Encourage coaches, teachers, parents, and other adults to set good examples.

(Bodinger-DeUriarte & Sancho, 1992; CDC, 1992; Ditter, 1988; Gaustad, 1991; Gregg, 1992; Greenbaum, Gonzalez, & Ackley, 1989; The Killing Grounds, 1991; NSSC, 1989, 1990b; Prophet, 1990; Scrimger & Elder, 1981)

One way to approach violence prevention is through classroom management practices. In addition to helping promote nonviolent behavior, the following strategies recommended by the California State Department of Education (1989) help foster academic achievement:

• Integrate students of all academic levels whenever possible.

• Use cooperative learning procedures and make the development of each student's self-esteem a primary objective of cooperative experiences.

• Involve students in classroom management procedures.

• Encourage parent participation in class activities.

• Require regular homework assignments to reinforce learning and provide the opportunity for students to practice personal responsibility.

• Keep class size small whenever possible.

Another way to prevent violence is by paying special attention to aggressive behavior in young students, such as school bullies, whose conduct may eventually lead to more violent behavior. Because these children often lack social and reasoning skills, do not know how to control anger, and tend to be more self-centered than their peers, they need to be taught how to interact more successfully with others. This instruction might range from simple skills, such as how to start a conversation, say "thank you," compliment someone, or ask for help, to much more complicated skills, such as coping with failure or embarrassment, reacting appropriately to an accusation, or setting personal goals (Eron, 1987). Another effective strategy with aggressive young students is to pair them with older students in social or academic settings; those who are bullies in their peer group are more likely to be willing "followers" among older students (Hoover & Hazler, 1991).

School and Community Service Projects

School and community service projects also offer students viable alternatives to violence. Through these projects, students perform beneficial services for their school or community through activities ranging from painting scenery for a school play to doing chores for the elderly. Community service projects are sometimes integrated with academics through service-learning units in which students discuss or write about their community service activities as part of their regular studies. Some schools incorporate community service into their regular curricula. For example, graduation requirements for students in Atlanta, Georgia, and the state of Maryland include 75 hours of service to the community (Elkind, 1988).

Designed to promote self-esteem, citizenship, and other qualities, school and community service also helps prevent violent behavior by

• enhancing students' sense of empowerment as they "give something back" to the community;

• encouraging students to care about others and behave accordingly;

• helping students develop problem-solving, social, and employment skills;

• fostering interaction among students from different racial, socio-economic, and cultural backgrounds; and

• providing students opportunities to give help to and receive help from peers (Follman et al., 1992).

In one type of service project that has gained popularity across the country, older at-risk students tutor and act as mentors for younger at-risk students. If the older students are properly trained and the program is well structured and monitored, both the older and younger students benefit. Not only do both make better grades, but many programs report improved attendance and few disciplinary referrals as well.

Counseling

Counseling is often necessary both for the assailant and the victim in cases involving violence. Forms of counseling include simply providing a "time out" and an opportunity to talk with someone, offering individual or group sessions to discuss problems, working to modify behavior and producing contracts for doing so, or offering educational or therapeutic sessions and seminars. As part of their violence contingency plans, schools and districts should make advance arrangements with local psychologists, therapists, psychologists, counselors, and others with special experience in dealing with violent offenders, victims, the grieving process, and violence prevention. These experts can be called on short notice in the event of a crisis and can also provide long-term support.

Character Education

Students who cannot follow rules do poorly in school and often disrupt the education of others (McKelvey, 1988). Since some children lack the social skills and self-esteem necessary for appropriate behavior, schools must often take an active role in children's character education. Schools must teach students how to interact positively with others, preparing them for responsible citizenship as adults.

The Character Education Institute identified a list of 15 values that they have determined to be shared by cultures around the world: honesty, truthfulness, justice, tolerance, generosity, kindness, helpfulness, honor, courage, conviction, citizenship, freedom of speech, freedom of choice, the right to be an individual, and the right to equal opportunity and economic security (Grossnickle & Stephens, 1992). Teachers can foster the development of these values by modeling them in school and classroom activities, and by teaching students how to resolve disputes, make good decisions, and work cooperatively with others.

> Schools must teach students how to interact positively with others, preparing them for responsible citizenship as adults.

One type of character education that has been used successfully by schools across the nation is values education. Through values clarification, students discuss their belief systems with their peers and teachers and learn to recognize beliefs that are incompatible with nonviolence. Students are also taught the importance of abiding by laws, accepting other cultures, and resolving conflicts peacefully. Designed to avoid indoctrinating students with one set of beliefs, values clarification guides students in developing a better understanding of their personal and family values.

Teachers can also help students develop a sense of personal and social responsibility through character education. Lessons on accountability for one's actions, patience and delayed gratification, consequence-guided decision making, and knowledge gained from failures as well as successes may be especially beneficial in countering the development of a "culture of impulse" (Grossnickle & Stephens, 1992).

According to Grossnickle & Stephens (1992), one way in which schools may emphasize character education in their educational agenda is to reinstate the "other side of the report card"—those measures that were once used to reflect a student's non-academic progress in social and classroom settings. Such measures typically included:

> **Students are taught to settle disputes by going through the process of conflict resolution, which typically includes active listening, acceptance of others' viewpoints, cooperation, and creative problem solving.**

- being courteous,
- playing and working well with others,
- following school rules,
- respecting the property of others,
- coming to school prepared,
- using careful methods of work,
- completing work on time, and
- observing traffic and safety rules (p. 31).

Conflict Resolution

Just as we cannot expect children to read without first showing them how, we cannot expect them to peacefully resolve their conflicts without instruction. In far too many families, children have no effective role models for conflict resolution; they react violently to stressful situations because that is what they see at home. Accordingly, many schools are establishing formal conflict-resolution programs. Conflict resolution involves teaching students how to resolve disagreements nonviolently by working together to arrive at mutually acceptable compromises (Inger, 1991). Students are taught to settle disputes by going through the process of conflict resolution, which typically includes active listening, acceptance of others' viewpoints, cooperation, and creative problem solving. Children, starting as young as age five or six, are taught that preventing violence and resolving conflict is a "win-win" proposition. The following steps are usually involved in a "win-win" conflict resolution:

1. Define the problem with mutual agreement on circumstances.
2. Generate possible solutions.
3. Evaluate solutions and eliminate inappropriate ones.
4. Negotiate the most mutually acceptable solution.
5. Determine how to implement the decision.
6. Assess how well the solution solved the problem (Perry & Duke, 1978, p. 85).

Students can either practice the conflict-resolution process when settling their own disputes, or teachers, parent volunteers, or students can be trained as mediators to help disputants resolve their conflicts. In schools with conflict-resolution programs, students report feeling better about themselves and safer at school, teachers report fewer fights and more caring student behavior, and conflicts are handled more quickly and remain resolved. Peer mediation has been especially effective in dealing with bullying behavior (Olweus, 1987). Many schools are finding that some of the best peer mediators are students who had previously been considered troublemakers (Inger, 1991); given the opportunity to contribute meaningfully to school activities, these students develop a sense of importance while reinforcing skills that can be used when they find themselves in conflict with others.

3. COLLABORATING WITH OTHER PROFESSIONALS
Developing solutions to the social problems that affect the safety of a school requires expertise often far beyond that of educators. California State Department of Education, *Safe Schools: A Planning Guide for Action,* 1989

In planning activities and implementing strategies to reduce violence, schools should seek the assistance and expertise of other organizations. Too often, the comprehensive needs of children and youth go unmet due to a lack of interagency collaboration, and the blame for failure gets passed from one agency to another. For example, principals often blame the juvenile justice system for their problems with violent students, but admit that they know little about the system, how it operates, or how to work it (Reaves, 1981). At the same time, law enforcement officials are frustrated by school policies that place disruptive youth out on the streets. Schools can take the lead in seeking to establish collaborative relationships with other agencies so that violence can be reduced, education can be enhanced, and children can be successful.

Schools need to establish and maintain an ongoing relationship with police.

While the most important collaborative relationship for addressing school violence is between the school and local law enforcement agencies, other agency representatives, including social service providers and policymakers, should also be involved in efforts to reduce and prevent violence among young people.

Collaborating with Law Enforcement

Instead of just calling on police during a crisis or violent incident, schools need to establish and maintain an ongoing relationship with police. This relationship can be initiated by school or district administrators and might begin with an introductory meeting at which both parties brainstorm ways they can help one another. If the police precinct has a public relations officer, he or she can be invited to make the initial visit to the school and talk with principals and other school staff. As collaborative strategies develop, the school and police department will need to establish specific policies regarding each organization's roles and responsibilities in working together (Gaustad, 1991).

Blount (1986) recommends that the principal designate as the "police liaison" that staff member who is directly responsible for maintaining discipline in the school. He or she would receive all reports from students, staff, and parents of suspected or actual violent behavior, and would make all school requests for police assistance or information. Communication from the police liaison would go to a school liaison officer designated by the police department. Together, and in consultation with the school safety committee, these two professionals could establish procedures for sharing information about potential crises, discussing trends in school violence, and reporting criminal incidents to the police (Blount, 1986). School administrators and directors of school security have found that police officers who have some college education, experience working with youth in the past, and good communication skills are usually the best choices for school-police partnerships (Gaustad, 1991).

The U.S. Department of Justice (1986) suggests that schools and law enforcement agencies can assist one another by

• sharing information on the frequency and proportion of crimes in schools in relation to the same types of crime committed in the community;

• jointly defining offenses and deciding which acts should be addressed cooperatively;

• jointly reviewing policies and procedures for handling students who commit crimes in schools, including guidelines for police entering a school, interviewing students and staff, and making an arrest on school grounds; and

• jointly participating in planning and implementing programs to prevent school crime and student behavior (pp. 61–62).

> **As students become more comfortable relating to law enforcement officers, their appreciation for them and the laws they enforce will increase.**

A benefit of collaborations between schools and police is that officers have the opportunity to develop positive relationships with students through class presentations and friendly interaction on a daily basis. According to Greenbaum, Gonzalez, and Ackley (1989), as students become more comfortable relating to law enforcement officers, their appreciation for them and the laws they enforce will increase. Students are, therefore, more likely to report suspicious activity in the school or community when they have gotten to know the police officers through nonconfrontational situations (Gaustad, 1991).

Law enforcement officials also have great potential as mentors and guides for students who may be or are likely to get into trouble. There have been a number of cases in which police officers have helped former gang members turn their lives around by listening to their problems, treating them as equals, helping them set goals, assisting them in finding jobs and getting to know their families (Gaustad, 1991). When informing parents and community members about the full-time or occasional presence of police officers on school campuses, such positive results should be highlighted to assure parents that the presence of law enforcement at school does not necessarily mean that there are serious problems (Gaustad, 1991).

Collaborating with Other Agencies
Other collaborative relationships can help schools reduce violence by ensuring that students' basic needs are being met. School staff may wish to contact the following professionals:
   • social service providers (counseling, conflict resolution, parent education)
   • early childhood specialists (social skills, dealing with bullies, identifying child abuse)
   • mental health/family counselors (counseling, therapy in aftermath of violence)
   • medical practitioners (recovery after violence crisis; describing effects of weapons on the body)
   • court judges and probation officers (legal ramifications of violence)
   • parks and recreation department representatives (constructive activities as alternatives to violence)
   • staff of state departments of education, health, and human resources (technical assistance, materials, financial assistance)

Each organization can identify one or more key contact persons that school staff can call to discuss collaborative strategies or to work together on behalf of a particular student. These collaborative relationships might net the following results:
   • a resource guide of educational social, and community-based services for students and their families
   • guidelines for hiring, training, pay, and employment of school security guards
   • creation of a task force to design a comprehensive plan of action for reducing gang activity in the community
   • summer activities for youth
   • linkages to early childhood education programs so that the message of nonviolent behavior is initiated at the beginning and reinforced throughout a student's school career (California State DOE, 1989; Gaustad, 1991; Governor's Task Force, 1979; Kean, 1981, Prophet, 1990)

Collaborative relationships may also result in political power that can be used to influence policies to prevent and reduce violence. Table 11 recommends some policy targets. For more information about developing collaborative relationships among human service providers, addressing confidentiality issues, and meeting students' and families' service needs, educators can refer to SERVE's publication, Interagency Collaboration (Kadel, 1992).

Table 11
Policies, Programs, and Legislative Initiatives
for Reducing School Violence

- Laws that prohibit carrying concealed weapons, that make it harder to buy and sell guns, and that increase criminal penalties for non-compliance
- Policies that establish "Safe School Zones" with stiffer penalties for selling weapons or drugs within 1,000 feet of a school
- Policies that automatically transfer from juvenile to criminal court cases of minors above age 14 charged with possessing or using a weapon on school grounds
- Laws that penalize adults when their weapons are found in a minor's possession
- Stiffer penalities for assaults on school staff or on school grounds
- Smaller schools and/or scheduling policies that reduce teacher-student ratios
- Increased funds for programs aimed at preserving and strengthing the family unit
- Legislation (such as California's constitutional amendment) affirming students' and staffs' right to a safe school

(CDC, 1992; Gaustad, 1991; Gottfredson, 1983; Hranitz & Eddowes, 1990; NSSC, 1990b)

---

4. INVOLVING AND EDUCATING PARENTS AND THE COMMUNITY

Violence is everyone's problem. Parents and community members must, therefore, be enlisted to reinforce lessons learned at school, help with activities that promote family and neighborhood unity, alert officials when there is a potential for violence, and work to reduce violence in the community as well as the school.

The foundation for good discipline begins at home. Parental discipline guides children toward acceptable behavior and teaches them to make wise and responsible decisions. Further, proper discipline helps transmit parents' and society's values. To extend discipline to school, it is important that parents support school rules and let their children know that they are expected to follow those rules.
A. Rapp, F. Carrington, and G. Nicholson, *School Crime and Violence: Victims' Rights,* 1992

Parents usually want the best for their children. An inability to cope with frustrations, stresses and their own needs often defeats their efforts at successful parenting.

Parents

Parents may need instruction in skills and strategies that will help them raise non-violent children. As Hranitz and Eddowes (1990) put it, "Parents usually want the best for their children. An inability to cope with frustrations, stresses and their own needs often defeats their efforts at successful parenting" (pp. 4–5). Table 12 offers suggestions for helping parents raise nonviolent children.

Parent involvement in anti-violence efforts gives legitimacy to school strategies and demonstrates to students that schools and families will not tolerate violence. Parents are more likely to get involved if they are invited to the school and made to feel welcome. Security procedures at the school should be no more threatening to parents than they are to students (NSSC, 1990a). The following list (Table 13) provides strategies and activities that schools and districts can employ to increase parent involvement in violence prevention efforts and also help prevent violence at home.

Table 12
Suggestions for Helping Parents Raise Nonviolent Children

- Provide parents information on raising and managing children, help in coping with family crises, parenting skills classes, and information on child development.

- Offer family and/or individual counseling, especially in cases of domestic violence or child abuse.
- Develop a "parents' guide" that describes parental responsibilities to prevent violence and legal responsibilities of parents whose children commit acts of violence in school. This information can be included with a listing of family services in the community.
- Inform parents about the effects of alcohol and drug use and tell them the signs to look for in determining whether their children are using drugs.
- Inform parents about gangs in the community. Send home explanations of dress codes that prohibit gang attire, and give parents tips for identifying signs of gang involvement.
- Encourage parents to inform school officials immediately if they suspect that their child is being bullied or victimized at school. Teach them to look for symptoms of victimization in their children, such as a withdrawn attitude, loss of appetite, or hesitation to go to school.
- Notify the parents of both victims and bullies about the problem. Help parents of victims develop strategies for their children to make new acquaintances and form healthy relationships. Help parents of bullies monitor their child's activities, praise prosocial behaviors, and use non-physical punishments for misbehavior at home.
- Discuss student fear and apprehensiveness with parents; be sure that they understand the importance of talking with their children about fear related to school and the need to reassure children in whatever way is necessary.
- Educate parents to discourage aggressive behaviors and encourage prosocial behaviors at home.
- Help parents teach their children to be assertive but not aggressive. Advise parents not to tell children to "fight back" but to stand up for themselves verbally. (The "fight back" message encourages violence and tells children that they are alone in solving their problems.)
- Advise parents that physical punishment legitimizes the use of force and should be avoided as a form of discipline.
- Encourage parents to monitor the television programs and movies that their children see and to limit or eliminate violent programming.
- Encourage parents to teach values at home and foster their children's social responsibility and moral character.

- Teach parents to talk and listen to their children. Emphasize the importance of investing quality time in their children.

(CDC, 1992; Eron, 1987; Gaustad, 1991; Governor's Task Force, 1979; Greenbaum, Turner, & Stephens, 1989; Grossnickle & Stephens, 1992; Hranitz & Eddowes, 1990; Wayne & Rubel, 1982)

Table 13
Strategies for Increasing Parental Involvement in School Efforts to Reduce Violence

- Include parent representatives on the school safety committee and school improvement team to help make decisions and recommend strategies.
- Hold some meetings at breakfast, lunch time, or during evenings to allow more parents to participate.
- Send a copy of the school's discipline cope to all parents and enlist their support in enforcing it.
- Create a parent telephone network to encourage parents to attend school events and meetings.
- Sponsor a "Generation Night Open House" in which students bring as many family members as possible to tour the school, meet staff, and socialize with other families. Have a photographer take family pictures and display them in the school.
- Call parents at work or send a brief note home to inform them about their children's accomplishments.
- Recruit parents and their children during the summer to help paint, clean, or repair the school and grounds.
- Provide transportation for parents to the school.
- Develop parent-student homework assignments with safety themes, such as comparing school or community crime problems today to those twenty years ago.
- Use parent volunteers to patrol schools and to keep an eye out for escalating conflicts at athletic events.
- Invite parents to be part of a School Crime Watch program, both as organizers and to provide security when needed.

(California State DOE, 1989; Greenbaum, Gonzalez, & Ackley, 1989)

Community

Recruiting community support for violence prevention efforts and other school activities can be difficult. Often, communities that are most affected by crime have enough difficulty dealing with neighborhood problems, let alone problems in the school (Menacker, Weldon, & Hurwitz, 1990). Another obstacle to garnering support is that a school suffering from crime and violence problems may also have a poor reputation in the community. In addition, since less than one-third of adults have school-aged children, most community residents have little interest in school affairs. On the other hand, violence has economic implications that may prompt community support for school efforts; property values are lowered when schools have poor reputations or when the neighborhood is plagued by crime and vandalism (Greenbaum, Gonzalez, & Ackley, 1989). Communities and schools need to work together for their mutual benefit, and schools can take the initiative to collaborate. Table 14 recommends a variety of strategies to involve the community in violence reduction efforts.

Communities and schools need to work together for their mutual benefit.

Gottfredson (1983) offers schools and communities these words of advice regarding efforts to reduce school violence:

• Don't expect spectacular or immediate results.

• Be skeptical of any claim that purports to be the solution to the problem of victimization.

• Try promising strategies for reducing school disruption.

• Monitor the implementation of programs and see that they really are implemented as planned.

• Evaluate prevention programs and make changes as needed.

• Expect some failures. Evaluations sometimes reveal that honest efforts do not always produce positive results.

• Learn from your experience, design a new program, and evaluate that.

• Make your entire school community aware that reducing victimization is everyone's concern.

• Persevere. Schools can take specific steps to reduce violence against teachers and students. Your firm resolve to create a learning environment that is safe for everyone is the first step.

• Celebrate and publicize your successes (p. 21).

Table 14
Suggestions for Promoting and Making Use
of Community Support

- Solicit advice from community residents on addressing school problems that they identify.
- Invite members of the community to visit the school and discover ways in which they can become involved.
- Develop a resource file of influential community residents—movers and shakers—who are known for their ability to shape public opinion; keep them informed about all school activities and projects.
- Include a representative from the community on the safe school committee; encourage a sense of "our" school, not "their" school, in community residents.
- Use the attention that school crime and violence receive to pressure local politicians and police forces to focus more efforts on the areas in which schools are located.
- Kick off community activities for violence prevention during America's Safe Schools Week, which is the third week in October.
- Ask news organizations to cover school safety activities and to emphasize the school's and community's efforts to reduce violence. Publicize violence prevention efforts through public service announcements, educational video programs, appearances on local news shows, posters, brochures, and other print materials.
- Develop a school safety fact sheet that is updated and distributed on a regular basis; include numbers and types of incidents, discipline actions taken, vandalism, and repair costs.
- Set up school information booths at local community events.
- Publish a newsletter from the principal and distribute it widely. Include information about school and community efforts to reduce violence as well as general information about school activities.
- Use the school's and/or district's emblem and logo to present a unified image in all publications and announcements.
- Ask businesses to allow employees time off to volunteer at schools or participate in school activities. Promote Adopt-A-School programs by local businesses.
- Encourage community organizations to use the school in the evenings and on weekends.
- Ask church leaders and clergy to help with violence prevention efforts at the school and with efforts to involve the community.
- Invite local government officials to school events.

- Encourage adults in the neighborhood to create and lead after-school youth clubs, community athletic teams, and other recreational programs.
- Recruit volunteer mentors and tutors from local colleges, universities, and businesses.
- Ask community residents to volunteer their homes as "safe houses" where children can go if they are threatened while walking to and from school or waiting at the bus stop. These homes can have signs in their windows designating them as safe houses; screen volunteers closely before including them in the program.
- Request that residents near the school take part in a nighttime school watch program and report any unusual activity at the school to the police.

(California State DOE, 1989; Ciminillo, 1980; Greenbaum, Gonzalez, & Ackley, 1989; Menacker et al., 1990; NSSC, 1990a, 1990b)

REFERENCES

Blauvelt, P. D. (1981). *Effective strategies for school security.* Reston, VA: National Association of Secondary School Principals.

Blount, E. C. (1986). *Model guidelines for effective police-public school relationships.* Springfield, IL: Charles C. Thomas.

Bodinger-DeUriarte, C., & Sancho, A. R. (1992). *Hate crime: Sourcebook for schools.* Los Alamitos, CA: Southwest Regional Laboratory, and Philadelphia: Research for Better Schools.

California State Department of Education. (1989). *Safe schools: A planning guide for action.* Sacramento, CA: Author.

Centers for Disease Control. (1992). *The prevention of youth violence: A framework for community action.* Atlanta: Division of Injury Control.

Ciminillo, L. M. (1980). Principal roles and school crime management. *NASSP Bulletin, 64*(433), 81–90.

Dade County Public Schools. (1988). *Procedures for promoting and maintaining a safe learning environment.* Miami, FL: Office of Alternative Education.

Ditter, B. (1988, Winter). Emotional safety and growing up. *School Safety,* 12–15.

Elkind, D. (1988, Winter). Disappearing markers and deviant behavior. *School Safety,* 16–19.

Eron, L. D. (1987, Fall). Aggression through the ages. *School Safety,* 12–16.

Florida Department of Education. (1992). *1991 Florida youth risk behavior survey report.* Tallahassee, FL: Prevention Center.

Follman, J., Kelley, M., Hammond, C., & Tebo, M. (1992). *Learning by serving: A guide to service-learning and other youth community service programs.* Tallahassee: Florida Department of Education, Prevention Center.

Gaustad, J. (1991). Schools respond to gangs and violence [Special issue]. *Oregon School Study Council (OSSC) Bulletin, 34*(9).

Gottfredson, G. D. (1983). School crime: From lunchroom larceny to assault on teachers, it's a broad problem, and it's big. *American School Board Journal, 170*(6), 19–21.

Governor's Task Force on School Violence and Vandalism. (1979). *Report and recommendations.* Lansing, MI: Author.

Grant, C. L. (1992, March 1). Reading, writing and weapons: Problems of the street spill into Dade schools. *Miami Herald,* 1A.

Greenbaum, S., Gonzalez, B., & Ackley, N. (1989). *Educated public relations: School safety 101.* Malibu, CA: National School Safety Center.

Greenbaum, S., Turner, B., & Stephens, R. D. (1989). *Set straight on bullies.* Malibu, CA: National School Safety Center.

Gregg, B. G. (1992, June 16). *USA Today.*

Grossnickle, D. R., & Stephens, R. D. (1992). *Developing personal and social responsibility: A guide for community action.* Malibu, CA: National School Safety Center.

Hoover, J., & Hazler, R. J. (1991). Bullies and victims. *Elementary School Guidance and Counseling, 25*(3), 212–219.

Hranitz, J. R., & Eddowes, E. A. (1990). Violence: A crisis in homes and schools. *Childhood Education, 67*(1), 4–7.

Inger, M. Conflict resolution programs in schools. *ERIC Clearinghouse on Urban Education Digest, 74,* 1–2.

Kean, M. H. (1981, April). School response to violence and vandalism: An urban district's perspective. Paper presented at the meeting of the American Educational Research Association, Los Angeles, CA.

The killing grounds: Can schools help stem the violence? (1991). *Harvard Education Letter, 7*(4), 1–5.

May, J. (1992, May 19). In tragedy's wake, students build esteem. *Detroit Free Press,* 10A.

McKelvey, C. A. (1988). Children who kill. *School Safety, Spring,* 12–16.

Menacker, J., Weldon, W., & Hurwitz, E. (1990). Community influences on school crime and violence. *Urban Education, 25*(1), 68–80.

Morganthau, T., Annin, P., McCormick, J., Wingert, P., Foote, D., Manly, H., & King, P. (1992, March 9). It's not just New York…Big cities, small towns: More and more guns in younger and younger hands. *Newsweek,* 25–26, 29.

National School Safety Center. (1989). *Student and staff victimization.* Malibu, CA: Author.

National School Safety Center. (1990a). *School crisis prevention and response.* Malibu, CA: Author.

National School Safety Center. (1990b). *School safety check book.* (1990). Malibu, CA: Author.

Olweus, D. (1987, Fall). Schoolyard bullying: Grounds for intervention. *School Safety,* 4–11.

Perry, C. L., & Duke, D. L. (1978). Lessons to be learned about discipline from alternative high schools. *Journal of Research and Development in Education, 11*(4), 78–91.

Prophet, M. (1990). Safe schools in Portland. *The American School Board Journal, 177*(10), 28–30.

Rapp, J. A., Carrington, F., & Nicholson, G. (1992). *School crime and violence: Victim's rights.* Malibu, CA: National School Safety Center.

Reaves, A. (1981). We let it happen, we can change it. *Thrust, 11*(1), 8–11, 36.

Scrimger, G. C., & Elder, R. (1981). *Alternative to vandalism: "Cooperation or wreckreation."* Sacramento: California Department of Justice, School Safety Center.

Speck, M. (1992, May). *Tokay high school proactive school safety plan.* Paper presented at the National School Safety Conference, Seattle, WA.

U. S. Department of Education. (1988). Improving student discipline. *Research in Brief, June.* Washington, DC: Office of Educational Research and Improvement.

U. S. Department of Justice. (1986). *Reducing school crime and student misbehavior: A problem-solving strategy.* Washington, DC: Author, National Institute of Justice.

Wayne, I., & Rubel, R. J. (1982). Student fear in secondary schools. *The Urban Review, 14*(3), 197–237.

Welch, G. (1989). How we keep our playground from becoming a battlefield. *Executive Educator, 11*(5), 23, 31.

What We Can Do About Gangs

by Mary Lynn Cantrell

It's easy to recognize that gangs are a present day phenomenon associated with real problems. It's less easy to determine what we can and should do to help youth faced with these realities. After more than three years of searching, this article will summarize some well informed suggestions from a variety of sources. The first section deals with what educators and schools can do, the second with how we relate individually to gang members, and the third with community and parent action that can be taken. The final portion will provide details on some useful resources the reader may want to pursue.

WHAT CAN SCHOOLS AND EDUCATORS DO?
Become Informed!
Talk to local police or others who know about:
> Names of gangs and territories,
> Identifiers—signs and colors,
> Members—numbers, names, characteristics, operational styles.

Ask the "straight kids"; they know:
> Who's intimidating?
> Who's recruiting?

Use Dress and Discipline Codes Knowingly.
Dress codes should exclude gang identifiers.

From *Journal of Emotional and Behavioral Problems: Reclaiming Children and Youth*, vol. 1, no. 1, p. 34–37, Spring 1992. Reprinted with permission.

Several New Orleans public schools have adopted school uniforms for all students there, avoiding many problems. They report that uniforms avoid students' either wearing gang colors or flaunting expensive clothing earned from illicit activity.
- Don't allow students to "represent" in school.
- Prevent and report "recruiting."
- Confiscate beepers and headphones.
- Develop clear assault and weapons policies.
- Report assault and weapons offenses.

Declare and Make the School A "Neutral Zone" for Gangs.
- Make policies public and repeat them when needed.
- Search for and destroy graffiti.

Take a stand against violence, and work to establish among students a school norm that supports that stand. One school secured anti-violent pledges from students, giving them group support for individually taking nonviolent stances in trouble-some situations.

> Take a stand against violence, and work to establish among students a school norm that supports that stand.

Anti-Gang Curriculum
More such materials are becoming available to educators. For example, in 1982 the Paramount California Schools began using a curriculum which includes:
Showing the reality of the gang lifestyle,
Demonstrating alternatives to the gang lifestyle,
Developing self esteem,
Providing models for dealing with peer pressure,
Giving drug abuse information,
Informing about the consequences of criminal behavior,
Exploring career opportunities.

Four evaluation studies were performed of the Paramount Plan Anti-Gang Curriculum. In summary, their results showed that before the curriculum, about 50% of students were undecided about joining; after the curriculum 90 to 98% indicated unwillingness to have anything to do with a gang. Such a curriculum must effectively deglamorize the gang lifestyle and provide realistic alternatives and support.

Include Other Important Student Curriculum Components, such as:
> Training in problem solving and good decision making,
> Pro-social skills training, values education,
> Non-violent conflict resolution methods and practice,
> Education in AIDS/STD prevention and personal safety,
> Incentives and support for academic performance.

Provide Relevant Inservice Training for Teachers and School Staff.
   • Gang related information and implications must be provided.
   • Bring in neighborhood leaders for joint problem solving.
   • Training in how to interact with gang members is critical.

> **Gangs place great emphasis on respect... Members are likely to return the respect given them by adults.**

WHAT SHOULD WE REMEMBER IN RELATING INDIVIDUALLY TO A GANG MEMBER?
Keep Cool.
   • Emotionality conveys lack of self control; take it easy.
   • Use humor if appropriate, but never "put down" or humiliate.

Show Personal Respect Without Attempting To Intimidate.
Gangs place great emphasis on respect. When walking through another gang's territory, members may tilt their hat or drape their sweater over the arm to indicate respect for the gang in that area. Members are likely to return the respect given them by adults. Life Space Intervention (Wood & Long, 1991) describes a useful framework for talking respectfully with youth in crisis.

Remember Not to Threaten.
Threats do not work. Gang members feel powerful and everlasting. Most members are likely to say what one Cleveland mem-

ber said when told he was likely to end up getting shot: "Not me; I won't get hurt." And if threatened with disciplinary action, they may well "up the ante" with greater threat or demonstrate that our threats are empty ones.

Be Someone Who Cares, but Don't Come on as a Therapist.
Relationships are important, but degrees are "a laugh" to gang members. If asked "What's happening?" they may tell about their concerns. If asked to talk about their feelings, they are likely to quit talking. Make your caring sincere; students have excellent "phoniness detectors." Listen well.

Point Out What Youth Pay for What They Get From Gang Membership.
The economic and protective benefits of gangs are difficult to dispute, but the loss of personal independence may not be clear to them. As Nick Long said to some PEP staff and students, "Once you're in a gang, they own you. You've gone back to slavery. Nothing in a gang is free, and no one in a gang is independent. Join a gang and they've won; you got beat!"

Don't Be Afraid to be Appropriately Assertive.
In the gang arena, fear invites intimidation. After a two year study of Ohio youth gangs, C. Ronald Huff (1989) put it this way:

"Contrary to much 'common wisdom,' teachers who demonstrate that they care about a youth and then are firm and fair in their expectations are rarely, if ever, the victims of assaults by gang members. Rather, it is those teachers who 'back down' and are easily intimidated who are more likely to be the victims of assault. During two years of interviews, not one gang member ever said that a teacher who insisted on academic performance (within the context of a caring relationship) was assaulted. Such teachers are respected far more than those perceived as 'weak,' and 'weakness' generally represents a quality to be exploited by gang members in an almost Darwinian fashion, much as they select targets on the street." (p. 531)

Many individuals lack assertive responses in situations where they are needed, rather, they progress from passive to aggressive behavior, both of which are nonproductive. If appropriate assertiveness is a problem for you, obtain some assertiveness training. But remember that being assertive does not mean acting tough. Acting tough presents a challenge for counter-aggressive action from students, and only makes things worse.

Use the Conflict Cycle (Long, 1979) to analyze behavior in a situation and to choose how we should respond so as not to escalate a problem. The Conflict Cycle suggests we try to understand the youth's view of himself and how the world operates. Then we can better predict his feelings and interpret his observable behavior following a stressful incident. This information can help us to react in ways which do not confirm his expectations and thus avoid reinforcing his inappropriate behavior in that situation.

> **Students are more likely to cause trouble and less likely to cooperate if academic demands are either too high or too low for them.**

Don't Ask Them to Do Things They Cannot Do.
Asking a student to pursue an unrealistic goal is likely to blow an adult's credibility. We cannot ask a member (or recruit) to leave (or not join) a gang where following our advice will probably get him killed. We may help him find ways to minimize his involvement and to seek other support.

Likewise, when setting academic expectations, we must make sure tasks are feasible for individual students and provide face-saving assistance where it is needed. Students are more likely to cause trouble and less likely to cooperate if academic demands are either too high or too low for them.

Allow Students Choices Which Enable Them to Save Face.
Maintaining the respect of their peers and, therefore, their self respect are constant primary objectives of gang members. Any other person who humiliates them is violating their integrity and therefore creating enemies.

WHAT CAN CITIZENS AND PARENTS DO?
Citizens Can Join Each Other to Act on Their Concerns about Gangs.
A great deal can be done together, but action requires unity and courage. A Chicago Police Department paper says, "Remember

this—a street gang is only as strong as the community or neighborhood permits it to be." But remember, the first step in solving a problem is acknowledging that there is a problem. Community awareness is a critical first task if you expect to bring people together to meet a need.

Contact with sources of gang information (like those described in this issue) can provide leads to places where citizen action has paid off. For example, the city of Paramount, California, paired its anti-gang school curriculum with neighborhood meetings for parents—providing parents and citizens with information, resources, support, and positive contact with law officers. Cleveland, Ohio, has established a gang hot line for anyone with a gang-related question or concern. A wide variety of information or community resource contacts can be obtained through the hotline.

> A street gang is only as strong as the community or neighborhood permits it to be.

Community agents can assist an individual in relocating if moving is what is required to leave a cult or gang. If asked, individuals and groups in the community may well agree to fund action which helps a youth or family escape cult or gang entrapment. Some communities have plastic surgeons who volunteer their services to remove gang or cult identifying tattoos for individuals seeking to leave the group.

High risk target areas can be identified by locating the zip codes where there are disproportionate numbers of prison commitments, correctional placements, mental health residential placements, and numbers on public assistance. In order to reduce the vulnerability of these areas to gangs, services should be provided which strengthen families and social institutions and which improve job opportunities. Organize campaigns to call or write local or national congressmen; inform them and let them know what you expect.

Neighborhood individuals, churches, community agencies, and social groups can work together with schools, parents, and law enforcement agencies. A note of warning from a Chicago Police officer—members of the Guardian Angels (neighborhood self-protective groups) can be gang "disciples" (low level involvement gang members), who can keep the gang informed and allow them access and protection when requested.

The influx of national drug-based affiliations has made the problem a national, state, and community issue. Citizens need to look for positive action which can be taken at each of these levels. One critical action is to inform your legislators, both about the problem and some of the helpful actions other communities have found.

Parents Have Some Options.
Caring parents can find hope in community support. They can be encouraged to:

• Spend time with their kids and find out what happens after school. Work to build and keep trust, a "You can tell me anything" relationship. (Such a relationship cannot last, however, if parents make demands they cannot enforce, such as "You are going to get out of that gang!") Make sure each child has someone to talk to.

> Parents can be encouraged to call police if they see anything suspicious (such as beepers, ammunition, or gang identifiers).

• Dress children in "safe" clothing; if they go to school wearing gang colors, they may be victimized. Don't purchase clothing in gang colors; often this includes college or professional sports team wear which has been "adopted" by a gang. Make sure parents are informed about the specifics of gang dress in their community.

• Check their home for gang signs and symbols: flipping mattresses can be a good idea. Parents can be encouraged to call police if they see anything suspicious (such as beepers, ammunition, or gang identifiers).

• Never permit youth to hold or attend non-chaperoned parties. Notify police ahead of parties. Parents can arrange for several male adults to be present. They can send out invitations to be collected at the door. They should check washrooms for hidden contraband, such as alcohol or drugs.

• Monitor what children and youth watch on television, and the movies they see. Parents can select some programs and place limits on viewing. They also need to talk with children about violence in entertainment media. Children need to discuss the fact with adults that violence in television entertainment is not reality. Violence as a means of getting what one wants needs to be actively de-glamorized by trusted adults, since it is highly glamorous as presented in most media.

Work with Your Police Officers, and Value Their Jobs.
Youth (and adults) learn to view law enforcement officials in stereotypic ways from the people around them, as well as from the media. Find positive ways to bring citizens into contact with police officers, and demonstrate productive problem solving with them about your community's needs. Let police know you are willing to join with them in acting preventively. Make sure your verbal references to law enforcement and your behavior with officers provide constructive models to others.

Let Media Sources Know What You Expect from Them.
We are inundated by movies and television with increasing violent and graphic "entertainment" and "news." Despite massive evidence of their destructive influence on our nation's children and adults, these still comprise the major portion of how our citizens spend their leisure time. Let your local stations, national networks, major movie production companies, and sponsoring businesses know what you think and what you want them to do. Contact them both as an individual and jointly with citizen groups.

Make Sure Prosocial Peer Group Opportunities Are Available.
Children and youth need identification, security, and activity which compete with less desirable options. Work to provide community youth organizations which have busy schedules of activities and prosocial adult models. Encourage Boy Scout troops, church youth groups, prosocial clubs, and arts or special interest groups to which students can belong. Use school facilities as community centers where productive social contacts can be provided, and make sure security is present. Keep kids busy with productive activity!

The Journal of Emotional and Behavioral Problems: Reclaiming Children and Youth is an interdisciplinary referred journal networking practitioners and policy leaders who serve children and youth in conflict with family, school, and community. Articles blend research with practical wisdom in a holistic perspective on the needs of young persons. Topics addressed in *JEB-P* include "Gangs, Guns & Kids," "Rage and Aggression," "Breaking Conflict Cycles," "Alcohol and Kids," and "Inclusion of Troubled Children." *JEB-P* is a quarterly publication available from the National Educational Service, 1610 West Third Street, PO Box 55, Bloomington, IN 47402. Call 1-800-733-6786 or 812-336-7700 for more information on subscriptions or submissions.

National Educational Service provides top-quality, timely information to educators and others who work with youth, concentrating on managing change and diversity not only of culture, but also in behavior, learning styles, and socioeconomic status.

REFERENCES

Materials from the Chicago Police Department. (1988).

Materials from Cleveland, Ohio's Task Force on Violent Crime. (1990 & 1991).

Huff, C.R. (1989). "Youth gangs and public policy." *Crime and Delinquency,* Vol. 35, No. 4 (October), Pages 524–537.

Long, N.J. (1979). "The conflict cycle." *The Pointer,* Fall 1979, Pages 6–11.

Wood, M.W. & Long, N.J. (1991). *Life Space Intervention: Talking with Students in Crisis,* Austin, TX: ProED, Inc., Publishers.

Violence and Our Schools: What Can We Do?

by Walt Landen

T he statistics are startling!
- One in 20 students will bring a gun to school at least once a month according to a U.S. Centers for Disease Control report, Fall 1991 (*Teacher Magazine*, January 1992).

- Violent assaults in schools escalated 14 percent from 1987 to 1990 (*Education USA*, October, 1991).

- 91,000 of the 2.2 million classroom teachers were attacked in 1987, according to a National Education Association poll (*Executive Educator*, October 1988).

- 28 percent of teachers in a National Center for Education Statistics Survey reported physical conflict among students ("Teachers Survey on Safe, Disciplined, and Drug-Free Schools," 1990-91; *Education Daily*, December 5, 1991).

- 25 percent of 12th graders admitted that they had been threatened with violence and 14 percent were injured in school according to the 1991 National Education Goals Report for 1990 (*Education USA*, October 14, 1991).

The headlines in daily newspapers are equally alarming:
"Schools Feel Impact of Armed Teens"—*Washington Post*, October 9, 1991
"Fear, rage follows school rape"—*Chicago Tribune*, February 15, 1992
"Why Are Children Turning to Guns?"—*Education Week*, November 6, 1991

From *Updating School Board Policies*, vol. 23, no. 1, p. 1–5, February 1992. Reprinted with permission.

"2 teenagers shot to death in Brooklyn school"—*New York Times*, February 27, 1992

America's violence has found its way into the schools and students, teachers, and education are suffering because of it.

NOT JUST AN URBAN PROBLEM ANYMORE

Though large urban areas still experience the greatest incidence of crime in the schools, a study by the Carnegie Council on Adolescent Development reports "...youth violence has no geographic limitations...It occurs much less frequently, but most often with greater impact, in suburban, small towns and rural areas." Reports from selected school districts indicate the numbers of students in rural areas disciplined for possessing firearms nearly tripled over a one year period. (U.S. Department of Justice, Office of Juvenile Justice and Delinquency Prevention, October 1989)

> ...youth violence has no geographic limitations...It occurs much less frequently, but most often with greater impact, in suburban, small towns and rural areas.

Many view the problem not as merely a school problem, but as a much larger community problem that is finding its way into the schools. Catherine Hobbs, vice president of the Montgomery County School Board, feels that "...what we are seeing in schools is representative of what is happening in society. Schools are not a haven of safety." This sentiment is reiterated by R. David Hall, president of the Washington, D.C., Board of Education. "Schools are not an island, they are a reflection of the community. You can't dump students in school and say 'you teach them different values' than they learned at home or in the community."

It's obvious violence is a serious problem. Understanding the causes is crucial to determining appropriate solutions. One apparent cause of violence is that children are exposed to it as a means for resolving problems. The news is filled with stories of individuals and groups who resort to violence for personal or political/social gain. Movies and television shows glorify the use of violence. Popular Saturday morning cartoon characters no longer just hit and yell at one another; they use modern and space-age weapons to maim and kill each other. And for increasing numbers of our urban poor children, violence and death are part of daily life.

We are teaching our children to be violent. *The Harvard Education Letter* has stated that experts believe "...the capacity for violence may be inborn, [however] children learn to be aggressive" (*The Harvard Education Letter*, July 1991). The best of intentions, in offering conflict resolution and self-esteem building classes in our schools, in providing counseling services to students and their families, and even in punishing unacceptable behavior will not be effective until we change societal attitudes and conduct.

As a society, in addition to teaching our children how to be violent, we are giving them the tools of violence. The national statistic that one in 20 students will carry a gun to school once a month is supported by a recent study conducted by the Iowa Department of Education that revealed that 23 percent of the 1,773 high school students surveyed carry a gun, knife or club to school. In many instances, we are supplying these weapons to our children.

These children are going to school scared—or they are not going at all.

The gun-per-residence ratio in the United States is 2:1 (*Eric Digest*, October 1991). Students have access to these weapons at home, and guns arrive at school for show and tell, for security, as power symbols, and to enact revenge.

A growing number of children say that they carry weapons as a means of self-defense. They are not the perpetrators, but the victims, of violence. These children are going to school scared—or they are not going at all. The *Set Straight on Bullies* survey, conducted by the National School Safety Center, indicates that some 800,000 students stay home one day a month out of fear (*CABE Journal*, March 1990).

The growing emphasis in education on the whole child and the linkage of services to meet children's multiple needs includes the safety and well-being of our students. When talking about the holistic approach to education, it is important to recall that the term is an all-encompassing one. A frightened child cannot learn any better than an unhealthy child.

THE SCHOOL BOARD'S ROLE

School Board members have an impact beyond their roles as education policymakers. As community leaders, Board members have the opportunity and responsibility to influence community standards and behaviors, particularly as these relate to their schools. The issues of violence and its control, and the availability and responsible possession/use of weapons are increasingly critical to the community's ability to provide a safe and secure learning environment for its children.

While the charge to serve as influences of public policy is part of the school Board member's mandate, primary responsibility remains the effective conduct of the education system. In that regard, there are steps that Board members can take to establish and maintain control of violence in school.

TAKING CHARGE

Recognition of the existence of or potential for violence is the first step. Admitting that we have a problem does not mean that we have, in some way, failed. Quite the contrary. Identifying an actual or possible problem says that we have the foresight, knowledge, and planning skills that are part of the portfolio of the effective school board member and administrator.

The sixth National Education Goal for the year 2000 acknowledges the problem of violence in the public schools and serves to direct our attention to its solution.

> By the year 2000, every school in America will be free of drugs and violence and offer a disciplined environment conducive to learning.

The community, in general, and the school staff, in particular, depend upon the leadership of their school Board to address and help solve the problem of school violence. Open discussions with community members and school personnel are the beginnings of the planning process. The need to involve everyone in a cooperative effort to prevent violence and provide a safe and secure environment in our schools is highlighted by a U.S. Department of Education survey that reported that 25 percent of the teachers polled had thought about leaving their jobs for safety reasons (*Executive Educator*, October 1988).

"All well and good," I hear you saying, "but what can/ should our school Board do, immediately and specifically?" Following are some recommendations for implementing a plan to take charge. First and foremost, if you do not currently have a school violence problem, do not wait until you do to develop the policies and procedures you will need. Metal detectors, drug and weapon-sniffing dogs, security personnel, and restrictive rules and regulations are not solutions—they are techniques to handle the problem on an ad hoc basis. School Boards may have to employ some, or all, of these measures to regain control, but they also need to develop an overall plan for school discipline and safety.

> **School violence is a community issue and demands community investment in developing effective solutions.**

DEFINE THE PROBLEM

Collect information and statistics so that you know what you are dealing with. Community involvement is an important element in assessing need and developing the means for meeting the need. Citizen advisory groups or task forces, composed of members of local business, religious, and civic organizations; municipal agencies; and parents can be valuable sources of information and support. School violence is a community issue and demands community investment in developing effective solutions.

Review District Policies

Are your policies updated and appropriate for current, as well as anticipated situations? Do they give clear guidance to the administration for providing a disciplined and secure learning environment? (See section on Developing Policies Regarding School Violence: Areas for Attention.) Do they reflect advice from legal counsel concerning the school's and school Board's liabilities? Be sure to check your state laws; you may be held in violation for failing to provide and maintain safe schools. Your Board needs to know what you can do to assure that all reasonable precautions have been taken.

Develop a Plan for Establishing Discipline and Maintaining Order

Your plan should include policies regarding searches and seizures, expulsion, cooperative agreements with law enforcement agencies. Dependent on circumstances, it might include installing metal detectors and/or hiring professional security personnel. The plan also should include provision of training for the entire school staff in how to deal with a variety of emergencies. Fire drills and safety procedures are not adequate in today's schools. Training in recognizing and responding to danger signals, good communication systems/arrangements within the school, and clear understanding of each person's responsibility in a crisis are vital.

> Classes emphasizing conflict resolution skills can give students the capacity to solve problems logically and peacefully.

Cultivate an Emotionally Healthy School Environment

Get to know, and encourage your administrators to know, the schools' staff and students. Provide the support and education/training needed by both staff and students to resolve conflicts. Insist on fair, consistently enforced rules for behavior. Reward good behavior. And, at risk of mentioning the obvious, remember that a smile and a kind word go a long way.

DEVELOPING POLICIES REGARDING SCHOOL VIOLENCE: AREAS FOR ATTENTION

Curriculum

Curriculum changes can serve as a multi-faceted approach to dealing with school violence. Curriculum can be used as a prevention tool and as a means of influencing student knowledge and attitude. Classes emphasizing conflict resolution skills can give students the capacity to solve problems logically and peacefully, diminishing violent behaviors. Effective Alternatives in Reconciliation Services (EARS) is an example of a program that offers that ability. Developed in New York City, this program is designed to encourage talking rather than fighting. The program works much like labor union negotiations, in that students who have disputes meet with specially trained student mediators and talk out their differences (*New York Times*, December 26, 1990).

A comparable program, "Violence Prevention Curriculum for Adolescents," generated by Deborah Prothrow-Stith, instructs students in "...anger management and nonviolent problem-solving techniques" (*Eric Digest*, October 1991). Curriculum also is being used to educate students about the dangers of substance abuse, a frequent cause of violence. Drug Abuse Resistance Education (DARE) is a popular program that involves police officers who have been trained for classroom teaching in instructing students on how to identify and resist the temptation to experiment with drugs and alcohol.

Workshops for Adults

Adults who discourage aggression and support logical problem solving afford children a strong foundation in avoiding violence and physical conflict. In the **Beverly, Massachusetts, School District**, school and health service personnel recently presented a workshop entitled "Parents Need to Know." Parents and the community-at-large were encouraged to come and participate in workshops designed to provide information about and techniques for encouraging children to utilize problem-solving approaches.

Within the school inservice training for teachers and school staff might include site security measures, student discipline and classroom management, conflict resolution techniques, and implementation of character development curricula. Through effective school leadership training, principals and other administrators can develop the skills to effect changes in their schools and to enhance the positive elements in their school environments.

Extra-curricular Activities for Students

Academic and social clubs and school-sponsored athletics are excellent ways of increasing student participation and investment in their schools, as well as promoting desirable concepts like sportsmanship and the benefits of team/group activities. Developing after-school programs for latchkey students can provide guidance and structure for children who would, otherwise, be unsupervised.

School Boards may want to consider cooperative agreements with community groups to offer activities for students. What happens outside school comes to school. Therefore, we need to be concerned about the activities that students participate in during their out-of-school time. "Safe Streets," in Tacoma, Washington, is an example of a program developed by a coalition of school officials, police, and community leaders. Designed to attack the growing youth violence in the city, it was founded on the belief that "...the community can achieve success if its various elements work together with determination and good sense" (*American School Board Journal*, October 1990). Developing programs in conjunction with local business may allow high school students to be engaged in the working world and to learn about responsibility and potential professions. These programs should, however, be constructed and regulated so that in-school learning does not suffer.

> We need to be concerned about the activities that students participate in during their out-of-school time.

Clearly Stated Rules and Regulations

• *Dress Codes.* School boards are considering policies establishing dress codes for students and staff. In California, the **Oakland Board of Education** banned "...clothing and jewelry denoting identification of a gang; expensive jogging suits frequently worn by members and drug dealers, and all hats and headgear and clothing designating membership in non-school organizations" (*New York Times*, January 22, 1992). The **Detroit (Michigan) City Schools** have implemented a complete ban on expensive clothes and jewelry. **Baltimore (Maryland) City Schools** are experimenting with school uniforms. The **Dallas (Texas) Board of Education** has adopted a policy opposing clothing and grooming that is deemed distracting or disruptive. The policy gives principals discretion to judge what is inappropriate.

While dress codes remain controversial as a means of controlling unwanted behaviors, proponents suggest that these guidelines result in fewer behavioral problems and a safer academic environment (*Newsweek*, November 27, 1989). Even though the courts have tended to rule that students do not have a constitutional right to dress or wear their hair any way they choose, school Boards should be prudent in implementing dress codes. Policies must be clearly stated, issued with reasonable notice to allow students to comply, and allow for minimal due process before students are disciplined for violations.

• *Weapons Possession.* It may seem obvious that school is no place for weapons, but the statistics—and our classroom teachers—tell us that weapons are in schools. It is incumbent upon school Boards to state in their policies why weapons will not be tolerated, what constitutes a weapon, and what will result from violation of the policy forbidding weapons. Following is a concise policy statement suggested in NSBA's National Education Policy Reference Manual:

"The Board of Education determines that possession and/or use of a weapon by a student is detrimental to the welfare and safety of the students and school personnel within the district. Possession and/or use of any dangerous or deadly weapon in any school building on school grounds; in any school vehicle, or at any school-sponsored activity is prohibited. Such weapons include but are not limited to any pistol, revolver, rifle, shotgun, air gun or spring gun; slingshot; bludgeon; brass knuckles or artificial knuckles of any kind; knives having a blade of greater than two inches, any knife the blades of which can be opened by a flick of a button or pressure on the handle, or any pocketknife where the blade is carried in a partially opened position.

School boards might consider making their schools weapon-free zones.

"The possession or use of any such weapon will require that the proceedings for the suspension and/or expulsion of the student involved will be initiated immediately by the principal."

School Boards might consider making their schools weapon-free zones. Efforts to do so would ideally involve the school, home, community, law enforcement and health services. Strategies would include apprehension, prevention, intervention, education, counseling, and student and public awareness programs.

• *Search and Seizure.* Many school Boards have policies that allow locker, desk, and/or vehicle searches. Districts that implement such methods usually inform students that lockers, desks, and parking lots are the property of the school and are subject to search. Some districts advise students when a search will be conducted; some require the student's presence if an article is going to be seized. Search and seizure policies and procedures can indicate determination on the administration's part to control violence and may reduce the number of students bringing weapons and illegal substances to the school.

When developing policies that address this issue, it is a good idea to provide clear guidance concerning their use. Searches and seizures must meet the standard of "reasonable suspicion" or "probable cause." In the words of the courts, they must be reasonable in inception and scope. That is, are there reasonable grounds for suspecting that a search will turn up evidence of a violation? Are the search and seizure measures reasonably related to the objectives of the search, and not excessively intrusive? Before instituting these measures, be confident that they are warranted by the prevalence and seriousness of the problem, that there is a need for immediate action, and consider the value and reliability of the information leading to suspicion.

• *Graffiti.* A simple, but important means of controlling misbehavior is attention to symbols. Immediate clean-up of graffiti is one way to send a signal to students that the administration is strong and uncompromising in its position on vandalism. It also prevents conflict over potential gang territory. And, it says to all students and staff: We care about you and your safety, and we are taking steps to protect you.

• *Beepers and Pagers.* With the exception of those students who have severe medical problems requiring emergency pagers, or those who are members of volunteer rescue units, there would seem to be no need for a youngster to possess a beeper. Police officials maintain that more often than not, children with beepers or pagers are involved in illicit drug trafficking. School Boards can limit undesirable activities by adopting policies to ban these devices.

School Design

School design and facility use that are flawed can allow, even encourage, unwanted behaviors. School policy can address building deficiencies by restricting student congregation in "blind spots;" recommending random security patrol of problem areas, such as restrooms, locker rooms, and parking lots; and increasing physical security with fences, lights, or metal detectors. Perhaps the most effective, and the least costly, security measure is staff visibility: When teachers and administrators are seen throughout the buildings and on the school grounds, disruptive students are less likely to engage in inappropriate behaviors and everyone feels safer.

Reward Reporting

Encourage students to report weapons and other violations. Tips from students are among the most effective ways to detect weapons and drugs in schools and to be alert to potentially violent situations. Schools might establish a hotline or peer counseling program that would allow reporters to remain anonymous. Whatever the approach, it is important to try to change perception of individuals who report from "tattletales" to heroes [heros]. Teachers can play a significant role in developing a sense of responsibility among students to report weapons, and they can reinforce the idea that those who report weapons are actually doing themselves and everyone, including the students with weapons, a favor.

> **School policy should promote commendation of individuals for combatting crime and violence.**

It is part of the education and prevention process to continually send messages to all students that their fellow students and teachers are not going to tolerate behavior that is counterproductive to education. School policy should promote commendation of individuals for combatting crime and violence. When possible, public rewards for citizenship and/or bravery could be presented to deserving students and school personnel. When public announcement is not possible, school Board members and administrators can privately recognize those who have acted responsibly.

A FINAL WORD

Increased searches, metal detectors, extra security, and dress codes are extreme measures for extreme conditions. While they are increasingly necessary measures, they will not solve the problem of school violence by themselves. To be effective, we have to combine control and prevention. Choosing curricula, providing staff training, and planning for crisis management are integral components of a school violence program. And, in the end, sound policy development is a school system's best prevention and control mechanism.

Facing Up to Violence

by Pat Ordovensky

Violence has become news in the nation's public schools, but are school administrators getting the message?

In just two weeks last fall, these stories made the news:

Five students are wounded as gunfire erupts in a crowded hallway at Detroit's Finney High School. Three students are shot at the same city's Foch Middle School.

Albuquerque police confiscate guns and ammunition from a student's car after a shooting at Valley High School.

Chester (Pa.) High School shuts down after two days of student fights.

Police in riot gear break up a brawl at North Hollywood (Calif.) High School.

A 17-year-old girl at Ravenswood (W. Va.) High School fires an 80,000-volt "stun gun" at a classmate who had been calling her names.

The 14-year-old daughter of a school board member in Atoka, Okla., is suspended for bringing a gun to school.

Violence has become news in the nation's public schools. A Florida survey finds school crime up 7 percent in one year. In a medium-sized Midwestern city, 15 percent of the students say they brought a weapon to school last year. The U.S. Justice Department's National Crime Survey shows teenagers are more than twice as likely to be victims of violent crime as anyone else.

Are school administrators getting the message? Do they understand they have a problem crying for attention? Are they trying to find solutions? The answers depend on whom you ask.

From *The Executive Educator*, vol. 15, no. 1, p. 22–24, February 1993. Reprinted with permission.

Most administrators surveyed by *The Executive Educator* and Xavier University this year say violence is increasing in the school districts next door, but fewer than half admit the problem is growing in their own school or district.

"Aren't blinders wonderful?" says Peter Blauvelt, security chief in Prince George's County, Md., and chairman of the National Association of School Safety and Law Enforcement Officers. He says many administrators are "going through a period of denial," refusing to accept the presence of violence in their schools.

"I'll give workshops on the issue," says Blauvelt, "and they'll sit there in the audience and say, 'Thank God I don't have that problem.' And then it happens in their school, and they call me and say, 'How do I deal with this?'"

PERCEPTION GAP

The U.S. Education Department finds a crime perception gap between administrators and teachers. In surveys of both groups, the department reports higher percentages of teachers than principals say they have problems with student violence, weapons, robberies, verbal and physical abuse, vandalism, and racial tension. For example, 22 percent of the nation's teachers say vandalism is a problem in their school; only 11 percent of the principals agree.

> Most administrators... say violence is increasing in the school districts next door, but fewer than half admit the problem is growing in their own school or district.

"There is a wide disparity between what teachers think and principals report," says Bill Hardy of the American Federation of Teachers. Principals face "institutional obstacles to honesty," he says. "There is no reward for admitting problems, because if you have problems, you're seen as the cause."

Blauvelt describes the perception gap in terms of time. At his seminars on violence, he says, "it takes an hour to warm up superintendents to the idea that they have a problem. Principals take a half-hour. Assistant principals, five minutes. They deal in real time with real problems. The closer you are to a problem, the easier it is to know you have one and need help solving it."

If administrators are denying the problem, "they're stupid," says Jack Delaney of Fall River, Mass., past president of the National Association of Secondary School Principals. "If we have a problem, the worst thing we can do is deny it. We're doing no one any good, including ourselves."

Alex Rascon, security director in the San Diego schools and president of the National Association of School Safety and Law Enforcement Officers, says the denial mode is prevalent in small districts where "crime is just catching up to them."

> **The National Crime Survey estimates 3 million thefts and violent crimes occur on school property each year, or about 16,000 a day.**

"I feel sorry for them," says Rascon. "They don't know what to do. They don't have the training, the expertise to handle it."

Larger districts that have been living with crime for years have learned how to cope, he says. The San Diego district has hired its own police force, imposed a dress code to keep out gang-related apparel, even removed student lockers.

"Closing the lockers," Rascon says, "reduced tardiness, reduced conflicts—you had all kinds of fights around lockers—reduced the availability of contraband and weapons."

HOW BIG A PROBLEM?

A few months ago, a small sign appeared suggesting that perhaps things are improving on the school violence front. In an Education Department survey, 33 percent of U.S. teachers today say student misbehavior interferes with their teaching, down from 41 percent when the same question was asked in 1988. And 61 percent say school rules are consistently enforced, up from 50 percent.

But the problem, whether growing or shrinking, remains large. The National Crime Survey estimates 3 million thefts and violent crimes occur on school property each year, or about 16,000 a day. It finds 6.7 percent of teenagers have been the victims of violent crime compared to 2.6 percent of the population over age 19.

The Florida Association of District School Administrators, in the closest thing available to a crime census, found 61,842 school crimes during the 1991-92 year in the 60 of the state's 67 counties that responded to a survey. The superintendent group says that's a 7 percent increase in one year.

Almost half the Florida crimes—30,573 of them—were assaults. The survey also found 9,234 larcenies, 3,512 weapons violence, 2,418 drug offenses, 854 forced robberies, 593 motor vehicle thefts, and 329 sexual batteries.

> The school bully who gets away with playground harassment moves toward criminal tendencies as he or she grows older.

In a 1990 Education Department survey of 25,000 eighth-graders, more than 21 percent said they had seen weapons in school. A University of Nebraska survey in an unnamed medium-sized Midwestern city found 15.6 percent of high school students took a weapon to school during the 1991-92 year, and 6 percent said they did it regularly.

In the big cities, school violence has been around so long that the Council of the Great City Schools gave the problem little notice in a report on how its 47 member districts are coping with the national education goals. Measuring progress toward Goal No. 6, a Safe and Caring Environment, the council notes only that 86.6 percent of its members have some kind of program to reduce crime and gang activity.

"It's not just a little pimple on your face, it's a widespread problem across the country," says Lyle Hamilton of the National Education Association, which last month launched a national school safety program that includes a video and print materials to alert schools to the scope of the problem and offer suggestions on coping. "Some tend to ignore [violence] and say it's not happening here," says Hamilton. "But it's there, and it will explode some day."

Many students "face daily decisions regarding high-risk situations," says *School Safety*, a newsletter of Pepperdine University's National School Safety Center in Westlake Village, Calif. "Plotting a hallway route becomes a matter of survival. Attending class depends upon the presence or absence of weapons carriers. To use or not to use the rest room replaces the decision to memorize or not to memorize Hamlet's soliloquy."

The problem no longer is confined to high schools but has passed through middle schools and is working its way into elementary schools, says security chief Blauvelt. Crack babies, he says, are coming to school with unpredictable and often uncontrollable behavior. The school bully who gets away with playground harassment moves toward criminal tendencies as he or she grows older.

"Elementary principals rarely attend [school security] workshops," he says. "They tend to confuse violent behavior with discipline problems."

ON THE FRONT LINES

Superintendents, some of whom concede they've gone through periods of denial, now generally say they are aware of the problem and either are dealing with it or have plans to meet it when it arrives.

"There was a period of denial among my colleagues in Texas, but now we are dealing with the issue," says Wayne Blevins, who left a superintendency in the Houston suburbs a year ago to become executive secretary of the Texas Teachers Retirement System.

"My concern is the weapons," says Blevins. "In a district of 30,000 kids, the last year I was there, I expelled more kids for weapons than in the entire history of the district."

Ask a student where he got the weapon, says Blevins, and he'll reply that he got it from his father or found it on the street or bought it at a flea market.

Wayne Doyle, superintendent in Monroeville, Pa., outside Pittsburgh, has issued metal-detecting "wands" to his building administrators and has hired a plainclothes security officer to spend the day in a red pickup truck parked outside the high school.

"He watches anyone who enters the school property," says Doyle. "His responsibility is to notify the office, by walkie-talkie, of anyone coming onto the property who could create a problem."

In Jackson, Miss., Superintendent Benjamin Canada has beefed up his security force, imposed a dress code, and banned beepers (often used in drug deals), and he randomly subjects students to metal detectors. Even so, he says, "Our children will tell you they feel safer at school than at home or anywhere else. School is the place where they know there is a teacher, a principal, somebody to stand up and say, 'You can't do that.'"

Echoes Lewis Finch, superintendent in Jefferson County, Colo.: "Even in our suburban community, an increasing number of our kids are safer at school than they are at home."

THE GANG THREAT

Talk to almost any superintendent about violence, though, and the conversation quickly moves to a concern that's spreading through school district offices from New England to California: the infiltration of gangs.

> School is the place where they know there is a teacher, a principal, somebody to stand up and say, 'You can't do that.'

"I can't think of any [Chicago] suburb not affected by the problem of gangs," says Paul Jung, superintendent in Des Plaines, Ill., and president of the American Association of School Administrators. "It hasn't reached the proportion we hear about in the cities, but we certainly have gang influence."

School executives across the country, working with police, identify gang-related colors and other clothing symbols such as baseball caps worn backwards and sagging shoelaces. Jung in Illinois and Canada in Mississippi say jackets of the Los Angeles Raiders football team and Los Angeles Kings hockey team can be gang symbols. Canada says the Jackson schools have a dress code that prohibits gang-related clothing. "We have no option," he says. "We send a message that it's not acceptable." Jung says he's confronting second-generation gangs. "You call the parents in," he says, "and find the parents are wearing the same [gang] colors as are the preschoolers."

Salem (Ore.) Superintendent Homer Kearns reports a school dress code is provoking complaints from parents in his district. "[They] say, 'My kid is not a gang member, and just because he's black and wears his hat backwards, you're harassing him," Kearns relates. It's a tough call, he says, as to "how difficult you can make it on a kid who may be nothing more than a wannabe."

Colorado's Finch handles the problem by giving building administrators flexibility to deal with it. "It's not just whether kids wear their caps backwards or have LA Raider jackets on," he says. "It's a combination of things. And that combination is up to the judgment of the principal or assistant principal."

In the Cincinnati suburbs, Mariemont Superintendent Donald Thompson says his school district has no gangs yet, but he has plans to deal with them when they arrive. He's heard from other superintendents that the Los Angeles-based Crips and Bloods gangs are organizing units across the country.

"We've heard comments by kids that they are from a Los Angeles gang or another gang," says Thompson, "as if they have an assignment to go to another territory that is not very well-populated with gangs and infiltrate. There is something going on out there."

Finch says educators aren't dealing with the central question of why gangs thrive. "These kids join gangs," he says, "because that's their family. They need someone who cares. They need someone to pay attention to them. They are somebody when they join a gang. The way we organize schools, sometimes, these kids are not getting as much attention and care as they deserve."

> These kids join gangs because that's their family. They need someone who cares. They need someone to pay attention to them.

San Diego's Rascon says he has from eight to 10 gangs in his district. He advises administrators to take a tough stance, including firm dress codes.

"Don't allow any clothes altered to identify a gang," Rascon says. "That includes hats, earrings, hair nets, anything that promotes the gang set. Don't let [gangs] claim turf. if you see T-shirts all the same style, say, "Wait a minute, we've got a problem."

Rascon frowns on peer mediation, a tactic used in many districts to defuse potentially violent situations by having students deal with disputes between students. "We don't want to put a student in the position of making a gang unhappy," he says. "I don't believe in allowing students to supervise students. It opens them to liability issues. If a student witnesses a crime, it puts him in a position where he must tell. We need well-trained adults."

We need more than that, says Ronald Stephens of the National School Safety Center, who offers a litany of steps a school district should take to alleviate the overall problem of school violence. He urges victim support programs, a climate that encourages victims to report crimes, close supervision of bullies and other potential troublemakers, and a curriculum on non-violent problem solving.

"Too often a victim feels that nothing will be done," says Stephens. "Our lack of responsiveness encourages kids to take things into their own hands. Violence is a tangible expression of unresolved conflict." Most important, "we need to make the public aware" of the scope of the problem, says Stephens, who bemoans the fact that no national records are kept on school crime.

"Safe school planning starts with good crime tracking," he says. "When people understand the scope of the problem in their schools, they're much more supportive of programs to address the issues."

Keeping Kids Busy
Key to Curbing Gangs

by Debra L. Williams

For many Chicago school-aged children, seeing acts of violence and gang activity is as normal as getting up in the morning.

Murder and violence have escalated dramatically in recent years and are directly related. Chicago has over 120 different street gangs. In some communities gang activity is so prevalent, children cannot imagine life without it. Gang members are role models and gang life is a career path.

One Chicago organization working to steer children away from gangs and stop the increase of violence on the streets is B.U.I.L.D. (Broader Urban Involvement and Leadership Development). A not-for profit community-based agency funded by the city's Department of Human Services, it is laboring to show children that there are other alternatives.

> There are always lots of people in my house who are in gangs. My uncle was in a gang. He got shot and died.

"B.U.I.L.D. has been around for 25 years," says Freddie Calixto, associate executive director. "We want kids to know that they have choices. These kids have family members who are gang members. Their brother or father is in a gang and they want to be in one, too. So what do we do? We bring in someone who graduated from their school and say 'Meet Jose, he graduated from here and he's a doctor.' Many of these kids don't know that is possible."

From *High Strides*, vol. 6, no. 1, p. 6, January/February 1994. Reprinted with permission.

The organization takes its message into the schools and the streets. Field coordinators give gang prevention workshops in Chicago public schools, work with youth who are already gang members, and with parents, teachers and community groups.

Middle school-aged children are especially targeted because, according to police statistics, gang recruits have been as young as nine years old.

"We work with fifth through eighth graders in 28 Chicago public schools," says Calixto. "These schools have a high gang visibility—active gang recruitment, drug activity and a high percentage of violence."

Calixto says the agency can tell which youth are at a higher risk for becoming gang members. In the beginning of the program students are asked to fill out a survey on themselves. One of the most important questions asked is what they do in their spare time. If there is no involvement in a boy's club, local YMCA or church and if their parents don't make them spend a major portion of their time at home, they are in trouble.

> Middle school-aged children are especially targeted because, according to police statistics, gang recruits have been as young as nine years old.

"When kids are hanging out in the streets, especially in these neighborhoods, they are vulnerable because they are going to be challenged," says Calixto. "'You don't belong to our group, so you must belong to the other group' is what they hear and then they are forced to make a decision about joining."

The field coordinators, some of whom are former gang members, conduct 16 sessions with the youth over three and-a-half months. They talk about what gangs are, gang activity, what can be done to avoid them and alternatives like education and careers.

Forms of violence, how to deal with it, drugs, controlling anger and emotions, communication and conflict resolution are also part of B.U.I.L.D.'s curriculum. After-school programs, mainly sports, are offered at some of the schools; children are urged to use existing programs at parks or other community organizations. B.U.I.L.D. also invites guest speakers to talk to students about special topics such as victims of gang homicides and prosecution.

"It's important that they hear from people like prosecutors who tell them how many young offenders they see and how much jail time they are now getting," says Calixto. "They have to know this is real life."

Many teachers see the program's benefits. "I can say the program has been very influential in reducing violence in our school," says Michael Jackson, a student conflict manager at K-8 Piccolo Elementary School. There has been no gang activity in the school since the program started teaching its curriculum last year. "We had little brothers of gang members who were actively recruiting in the school who stopped and eventually dropped out of a gang themselves," says Jackson.

His students are being taught to take responsibility for their actions, respect others and understand that gangs are not the way to go. B.U.I.L.D. also helped create a parent patrol system of about 20 adults, mostly men, who patrol around the school in the morning and when school is over. "They wear blue armbands and kids can easily identify them. Children feel safe coming to school, and our attendance has gotten better," says Jackson.

And what do the children say and think about it?

"There are always lots of people in my house who are in gangs. My uncle was in a gang. He got shot and died," said a fifth grader at Piccolo Elementary School.

"At first, students said they liked the program because they got to watch videos," says Calixto's brother, Heriberto Calixto, a field coordinator who is also an ex-gang member. "But eventually they get drawn into our message because I give it to them straight about what it's like on the streets."

"I like the program because it shows us why we shouldn't be in gangs," says fifth-grader Pamela Davis. "I don't like gangs anyway because they shoot people. I've had to lay flat on the ground and stay still until they go away."

"There are gangs near my home too," says another fifth grader, Rafael Rodriquez. "I guess we have to know how to deal with them which is what the program teaches us. I know I'll run away if they come near me."

B.U.I.L.D. also works with teachers on identifying gang symbols. Certain colors, haircuts, or the way gym shoes are laced or pant legs are rolled up are all potential gang signs that teachers and parents need to be aware of, says Jackson.

The program takes its message to the streets and works directly with young gang members on their own turf. Field coordinators get to know groups by drawing them in with sports; after rapport is established, they offer them alternatives such as jobs and education.

Still, Calixto says both alternatives are hard sells. "The schools they were attending don't want them back because they were disruptive. There is a long waiting list for alternative schools and vocational schools, which are expensive."

Jobs are hard to come by and, further, young men want one that pays well immediately, he says.

But Calixto and his brother count success when students say they'll never become gang members and they see these same kids keeping busy in after school programs, sports or other activities rather than hanging out on street corners: "That's success. It means they are not in the streets getting into trouble."

How to Help Gangs Win the Self-Esteem Battle

by Richard F. Arthur

I didn't know anything about gangs until I worked at Virgil Junior High School on Vermont Avenue in Los Angeles. There were members of three gangs in my homeroom who wore jackets to identify themselves.

Suddenly, I learned how deadly gangs could be when one student was killed while he walked through the tunnel under the street. Two others were killed near Echo Park and another one was killed near the school.

Because homeroom teachers were required to clean out student lockers, I had a key for all lockers. Usually, I found hard liquor and beer, but I also found various weapons such as knives, chains, and lead pipes.

> Suddenly, I learned how deadly gangs could be when one student was killed while walked through the tunnel under the street.

In 1959, I transferred to Washington High School where some gangs existed, but they weren't very active until my last year in 1966. I lived near the school and witnessed gang activities including drug sales.

In 1966, I transferred to the Watts Skill Center near 111th Street in Watts, which was opened after the Watts Riot. I worked with several gangs who were very active in this area.

Next, I transferred to Jefferson High School where gangs were also very active in 1968. Student unrest and tension ran high. As a community organizer for the school, I went into the community and tried to get gang members to come to school.

From *The School Administrator*, vol. 46, no. 5, p. 18–20, May 1989. Reprinted with permission.

SETTING GROUND RULES

In 1970, I became the principle of Castlemont High School in Oakland. Because the gangs were disruptive, I met with gang leaders and asked them to have a truce on campus. They kept their promise and made the school neutral territory.

I worked closely with all the churches in the area to help gang members. Unfortunately, we read about students being killed on a regular basis. However, I was able to help a few graduate and go to college.

During the summer months, I turned the school into a special vocational school. Many gang members attended. We used Comprehensive Employment and Training Act (CETA) funds to pay them for part-time work after school.

I also started an alternative school or street academy near where most of the gang members lived. The superintendent of schools, Marcus Foster, served as a member of the special school board. An inspirational leader, he was the motivating force behind my decision to take the principalship in Oakland.

Tragically, Foster was murdered by the Symbionese Liberation Army on November 6, 1973. He was shot as he left the school district office.

I rented a storefront for the street academy and placed several teachers and a counselor there. The students liked the school because they could walk there easily. I also allowed them to smoke and we had very few rules. Attendance improved. We allowed the students to plant crops in the back of the property and give the food to their families. Those who acquired sufficient credits were allowed to graduate with their class.

In 1975, I started a training and educational project in Hawaiian Gardens. The program was funded for three years and the city of Hawaiian Gardens allowed me the use of the recreation center for the program. Members of several gangs from Artesia High School in Lakewood enrolled in the program.

CETA FUNDS HELPED

I established classes and a recreational program that included boxing. We used CETA funds to provide job training and remedial education for those who needed it.

Some earned high school credit and returned to Artesia High School prior to their graduation. Some were placed in entry-level job positions. A few went to college.

Sadly, several were killed and others were convicted of various crimes. I cannot recall the final statistics, but we felt that, overall, the program was a success.

In 1980, I worked for Jobs for Progress in East Los Angeles and Van Nuys. I met with a large group of gang leaders and made a deal with them: Their members would receive training and jobs if they would make our school neutral territory. The arrangement worked—better than anyone could have predicted.

Theirs is a world of drugs, gangs, and violence. School may be the only hope for many of them.

Gang members were paid to paint over graffiti throughout the community. Some painted murals. Others worked to clean the houses and yards of senior citizens. Some were trained as auto mechanics or aircraft workers.

Others were taught basic reading and math so that they could take the high school equivalency exam and receive their diplomas. Some went to college.

This great program ended with the termination of CETA funds by the Reagan Administration in 1983. That is the year I returned to Jefferson High School as a teacher.

Many of our students live in an entirely different world from the one in which my generation grew up. Theirs is a world of drugs, gangs, and violence. School may be the only hope for many of them. If those who run our cities, counties, states, school districts, and nation do not act to help our students, I see only disaster ahead.

Ken Wibecan, an editorial writer with the *Long Beach Press Telegram*, recently wrote several insightful columns about why kids join gangs:

• "Drive-by shootings were originated by a bunch of guys with names like Capone, Nitti, Diamond, Siegel, and Dillinger, all of whom have subsequently become national folk heroes."

• "You are nobody if you don't get busted in the sweeps" by the police.

- They are "not old enough to vote or to purchase cigarettes. But old enough to be educated, which they are not. And old enough to kill."
- "These young folks have been shortchanged and they are making the rest of us pay for it."
- "High school graduates do not become gang bangers; it is as simple as that."
- "The teenagers are the middle-men in the largest and most profitable business in our nation, one clearly not minority-owned and controlled."
- "We may have already lost many of this generation. Let's not lose another."

We must decide as a nation whether we want to spend more for prisons, mental hospitals, adult illiteracy, and drug rehabilitation than on elementary school education. If we decide to continue the status quo, we should stop all the talk about gangs and drugs and learn to live with them. At least the kids could respect us a little more for ending our hypocrisy.

SEARCH FOR SELF-ESTEEM

I currently teach a college class for teachers that deals with gangs and drugs. As part of the course, I invite a psychologist, Rex Dalby, as a guest speaker. He emphasizes fostering self-esteem and caring to keep kids from joining gangs.

Dalby believes we "must start listening to young people and giving them an opportunity to talk to someone who cares. It can be a parent, teacher, counselor, policeman, janitor, or anyone who will listen."

Young people join gangs because they meet important needs that go unmet in every other aspect of their daily lives. The gang gives them a sense of security and structure that is also lacking at home. The gang is loyal while others in their lives are not only disloyal, they may even be very antagonistic toward them.

They feel most adults cannot be trusted because most adults won't listen to them. These kids feel they are worthless; they feel helpless; and they believe that everything is hopeless.

Someone who really cares can turn them around and head them in the right direction. They want discipline and a sense of direction.

ADULTS MUST CARE

Gang kids don't make it easy to like them.

I once disliked a gang kid because he disrupted my class every day; he swore too much; he drank alcohol between classes; he practiced extortion; he failed every class; and he hit the girls in his class.

Then I decided to visit him where he lived in an apartment building. His father had been beating him regularly. His mother was working and trying to make it on her own with five children. He was babysitting his four younger brothers and sisters. The sink was full of dishes. The kids were running in and out. They all looked filthy.

He was drinking a beer and he asked me if I wanted one. He told me that I was his favorite teacher and asked me how he could go about "making it" with one of the girls in the class. He told me he had been in a serious fight with "a stranger from another neighborhood."

Young people join gangs because they meet important needs that go unmet in every other aspect of their daily lives.

After that I couldn't hate him any more. Later, I attended his funeral. He never got a chance to go to high school or to have a date with that girl.

Everyone needs self-esteem. Gangs and drugs thrive where it's lacking. Unfortunately, many teachers may also lack self-esteem and feel they aren't treated professionally. Many feel they simply don't have time to give kids individual attention.

While everyone has occasional self-doubts, these kids feel that way most of time because everyone in their lives keeps telling them that they are no good and can't do anything right.

SELF-FULFILLING PROPHECY

Because many of these kids expect to fail at everything, including making friendships, they are pleasantly surprised at the recognition and sense of belonging gang membership gives them. Many are afraid of the future and do not understand the reasons we give them for going to college. These fears begin in the early grades and increase during the junior high school years when gang activities are part of their daily lives.

And some schools can be very negative places: "Don't do this; don't do that." "Take off that hat." "Don't be late to class." "Why didn't you do your homework?"

Just recently, for example, I asked a girl why she didn't do her homework.
She started to cry. Later, I found out that she didn't have a place to sleep the night before.

I got on another student who was a senior. Later, I learned he worked from 8 p.m. to 3 a.m. as a janitor to support his family.

Most teachers care. Most of us want to help kids to learn and to succeed in life. That's why we work with kids every day. But many of us are frustrated and angry because we believe that no one else cares.

We are angry when people keep talking about better schools but do nothing. We are sick and tired about "reforms" when we don't see them. Many of us only see more gangs, shootings, drugs, suicides, child abuse, dropouts, and kids suffering.

There is only one answer to stopping the tremendous increase in drug abuse and gang activities: All of us must care.

The Educational Needs of Children Living with Violence

by Susan E. Craig

Teachers are in a position to have a significant impact on the cognitive profile of children living with violence. Ms. Craig provides the details.

The decade of the 1980s proved that home is not always a haven against the harsh realities of life outside. For many, it is the battlefield where domestic violence claims its victims—battered spouses and physically, emotionally, and sexually abused children. For some children, family violence is so severe that it results in intervention by public authorities. For many other youngsters, it remains a secret destroyer that slowly permeates the fabric of the self and distorts the content of all relationships. The normal expectations of school and neighborhood are not waived for these children. However, the sense of competence that most children derive from interactions with teachers and peers often eludes them.

The nature of the relationship between family violence and student performance is difficult to assess. Early studies of parental abuse and child development often relied on samples of children who were already identified as disabled, making causal connections ambiguous. In some cases, the fact that a child has difficulty negotiating developmental milestones may trigger parental abuse. In other cases, the experience of violence in and of itself may result in a child's displaying learning characteristics that differ from those of children reared in less stressful envi-

From *Phi Delta Kappa*, vol. 74, no. 1, p. 67–71, September 1992. Reprinted with permission.

ronments. Either way, child behaviors that lead to academic frustration and school failure accompany histories of family violence.[1]

Since abused children most often remain in regular class-rooms, they must rely on the care of classroom teachers. Thus it is crucial to identify educational interventions that are responsive to their needs. This task can best be accomplished by combining our knowledge of educational "best practices" with our knowledge of the types of cognitive and social dysfunction exhibited by the children of abusive parents.

> **Child behaviors that lead to academic frustration and school failure accompany histories of family violence.**

Particular attention needs to be given to the impact of family violence on how children represent or encode material to be learned and on how they interpret and act on new information. These metacognitive structures, or "executive processes," determine a child's cognitive style and are influenced by environment and experience.[2] Abuse family environments influence children's problem-defining and problem-solving behaviors.[3] These behaviors, in turn, can affect both social competence and school achievement.

COGNITIVE AND SOCIAL DYSFUNCTION

Patenting styles that include verbal and physical abuse are frequently linked with reduced competence of children. Some authors draw a connection between abuse and deficiencies in the child's social/psychological development.[4] The majority link this type of parenting to a variety of neurological soft sign deficits (e.g., short attention span, impulsive behavior, heightened physical activity) as well as to impairments of intellectual functioning and language development.[5] Other than the effects of direct head trauma, most of the damage takes the form of aberrations in children's cognitive styles that hamper their ability to succeed.

Intellectual impairment

The ability to bring linear order to the chaos of daily experience is central to the cognitive processes tapped by academic pursuits. Developmental psychologists view this skill as the ability to develop sequential memory and ordinal positioning. Most children begin to encode events or memories in this manner by the time semantic language emerges.

Before the emergence of semantic language, memory is much like a series of snapshots that capture the essence of experience but may lack a linear sequence. This type of episodic memory continues throughout our lifetimes for events that "shock" us out of our sequential mindset, as in the death of a loved one or a traumatic injury.

Developing long- and short-term goals has little meaning to children who live in family systems focused on the "now," with little emphasis on past or future.

The transition to sequential semantic memory is most easily made in environments marked by consistent, predictable routines and familiar, reliable caregivers. In the absence of these factors, children may continue to encode new information episodically or not at all. Children raised in households in which rules and routines are subject to the whim of the parent may lack the consistency and predictability required to move easily into a more sequential ordering of the world. The result may be a learning style that is unresponsive to school environments that rely on sequential ordering. Developing long- and short-term goals has little meaning to children who live in family systems focused on the "now," with little emphasis on past or future.

The establishment of cause-and-effect relationships is another important cognitive process that children must develop in order to meet both academic and behavioral expectations of the school environment. Most children grasp this process during the sensorimotor period, through an active exploration of the world around them. They quickly learn that they can "make things happen" and, in doing so, establish the basis for developing a sense of competence and responsibility. They become the "locus of control" in their own lives—responsible, in some part, for both their successes and their failures.[6] Children living with violence often have histories of physical restriction and unrealistic parental expectations that inhibit their exploration of the world and their emergent sense of competence. An inability to anticipate the behavior of others or to change parental behavior toward oneself hinders the development of both competence and responsibility.[7]

An extended experience of perceived low impact on the world inhibits the development of such behaviors as goal-setting and delayed gratification. These skills, so important to school success, rely on a person's ability to predict and make inferences. Similarly, failure to establish an internalized locus of control results in an apparent lack of both motivation and persistence in academic tasks, as well as a resistance to behavior management techniques that assume an understanding of cause and effect.

Finally, living with violence inhibits the cognitive processes by which a child develops an awareness of the self. A metacognitive sense of the self as object is rooted in the cognitive processes of making choices and differentiation. In typical development, children have repeated interactions with the world that encourage them in the establishment of preference and perspective. Within a violent family system, indications of preference or opinion can tip the already precarious balance between parental indifference and parental aggression. As a result, the child learns not to express a preference until the mood of the parent can be ascertained.

> **Abused children often develop symptoms of timidity, fear of strange places, and a pervasive fear of taking risks.**

The impact on the self is simple yet profound. Children living with violence learn quickly that safety is best achieved through a "sensory muting" that allows them to mirror the preference of the caregiver at any given time.[8] The price children pay is an absence of feeling and a sense of incompetence that stem from an inability to define the boundaries of the self and thereby to experience self-control. This lack of differentiation limits all areas of development. For example, it can inhibit the child's orientation of self in space. This affects not only coordination and movement but also children's sense of control over their physical environment. Abused children often develop symptoms of timidity, fear of strange places, and a pervasive fear of taking risks. Ray Helfer and Henry Kempe describe this effect of growing up in a violent family as growing up to be "out of control."[9]

Social dysfunction

Closely related to the failure to perceive the self as an object that is constant across time and space and that is able to control its impact on the world are the types of social dysfunction associated with children who live with violence. Failure at self-individuation prevents children from differentiation between feelings and behavior. They are unable to objectify the self sufficiently to observe their feelings and make decisions about how to act on them. This inability fosters the development of reactionary behavior patterns and intensifies the sense of being out of control. In classrooms these children may appear inattentive and impulsive. In fact, they are perhaps overattentive—but to the wrong agenda. Their attention is directed toward interpreting the teacher's mood. Cues to "pay attention" further invalidate their perception and exacerbate their sense of dissociation from what they feel and experience.

Perhaps most important, lack of self-differentiation prevents children from getting their own needs met. Their attention has been directed toward meeting the parent's needs and trying to control the parent's behavior. They cannot risk the "luxury" of looking at themselves. It isn't safe. They fail to establish other people as agents of support or providers of what they need. Rather, the "other" is always a threat. Behaviorally, these children often vie for power with classroom teachers, since they know that they are safe, only when they control the environment. They do not like surprises or spontaneous events, which are perceived as dangerous or out of their control.

Language development

Abused children use language to keep other people at a distance.[10] Their communication style is gesture-oriented and is used to define the relationship between themselves and the speaker, rather than to convey meaning. They have difficulty focusing on the content of language. Chronic experiences of inconsistent, dangerous parent/child interactions cause children to closely monitor the relational messages they perceive nonverbally, rather than moving to the task at hand.

Deprived of an environment in which spontaneous speech is encouraged and physical involvement rewarded, these children often lack the requisite skills to initiate and sustain the day-to-day social events of normal school life. When family stress interferes with normal play time, the ability to take the role of the other or to appreciate another person's point of view may be seriously impaired. This condition may interfere with academic tasks that require the ability to solve a problem from a different perspective. Inferential comprehension, team sports, and estimation tasks may all be affected. Games and recess periods may become more stressful as rules become more complex and practice time more necessary for competence. Children may develop avoidance patterns of oppositional behavior and incomplete work as "face saving" techniques for getting out of play time. Though painful in themselves, these practices may seem safer to the child than the experience of failure before peers.

> When family stress interferes with normal play time, the ability to take the role of the other or to appreciate another person's point of view may be seriously impaired.

EDUCATIONAL INTERVENTION

The profile of children living with violence is comparable to Martin Seligman's description of learned helplessness.[11] Such children experience life as a series of things happening to them rather than as a process over which they can exert increasing control. Before they can be expected to function in an educational environment that assumes individual responsibility for learning, they must be taught that what they do actually affects what happens to them.

Management and instruction of these children requires educators to infuse the current curriculum with the consistency, predictability, safety, and sense of purpose that can accommodate the cognitive style of these children. Constructivist views of education, which make children active participants in their own learning, are important to the educational needs of children who live with violence. The lack of congruence between the life experience of these children and the reality assumed by public schools cannot be left unacknowledged. Life with violence leaves children without the internal control required to engage in independent inquiry in the absence of external support. For these children to be successful, teachers must orchestrate learning environments in which the discovery of competence is possible.

Current "best practices" offer suggestions on how to do this. Each of these approaches defines education as a process that involves active participation of both teachers[12] and students.[13] Teachers are responsible for structuring the interactions between the realities of children's personal lives and the expectations of the learning environment. In other words, they facilitate the discoveries that are to be made by providing students with the tools to make them. Emphasis on modeling, demonstration, and practice makes these "best practices" particularly responsive to the needs of children living with violence.

Lesson designs that incorporate the eight steps recommended by Madeline Hunter meet these children's needs for predictability and consistent routine.[14] Beginning each lesson with an anticipatory ritual allows time for the child to check out relational aspects of the interaction before content is introduced. It also identifies a clear beginning of the task at hand. Identifying the objective of the lesson and its purpose provides further grounding in the routine and allows the child an additional aid in focusing on the task. Active instruction and modeling provide a concrete representation of the task as well as auditory and visual sequencing of the content. Monitoring for understanding externalizes the type of self-management we wish for each student. Through the turn-taking and reflection encouraged at this stage, children experience control of the material and of their own interaction with it. Guided practice and summary activities extend this self-differentiation through reflection on what the experience was like. Within this structure, individual practice becomes an experience of competence, not failure.

Characteristics of the encoding processes of those children—specifically their tendency to think episodically—benefit from this type of consistent, rule-bound learning environment, with its clear demarcations of time and space. Further adaptations of these methods might include the use of pictures to indicate the beginning, middle, and end of tasks. Formal transition periods between activities will also facilitate the child's involvement in ordinal or sequential tasks. Learning activities that convey the "big picture" rather than many discrete facts will be more meaningful to this type of student.

Instructional approaches that actively involve students such as the cooperative learning model,[15] provide opportunities to play roles and take perspectives that may not be available at home. Cooperative learning's commitment to modeling the social skills required for the completion of tasks creates a sense of belonging for students who may otherwise be unclear as to what a specific behavior "looks like" or "sounds like."

> When students participate in experiences of group success, they have a mirror in which they can eventually observe their own personal competence.

The group problem solving inherent in the model allows students to speak spontaneously within a safe context, where alternative points of view can be shared without fear of retribution or humiliation. Self-differentiation can be encouraged through group activities that involve choice making and reflection. The use of group incentives for achievement is a powerful reinforcer of the relationship between effort and accomplishment. When students participate in experiences of group success, they have a mirror in which they can eventually observe their own personal competence.

There is a rich body of research on instruction in cognitive strategies: teaching students procedures that empower them to accomplish important academic tasks.[16] Strategy instruction highlights those characteristics of the learning environment that are most critical to completing tasks. It does not require the discovery of efficient tools for learning, but rather provides them to students who, lacking the dominant cognitive set, may otherwise fail repeatedly. This type of intervention is responsive to both the language and metacognitive characteristics of children living with violence.

Children living with violence often present many competing needs, so the first step is for teachers, related service providers, and children to discuss and set priorities. Once this has been accomplished, decisions must be made about the degree of participation that is expected from the student. Special education offers systems of assistance that allow participation in ongoing routines. Although the special education approach is most often applied to children with developmental disabilities, it is conceivable that this way of thinking may be beneficial to other students as well. For example, children living with violence may require additional support to complete the tasks of childhood.

Teacher assistance teams[17] and other types of pre-referral strategies help schools make decisions and develop programs that allow the successful participation of children living with violence. These approaches avoid labeling children as defective in some way. Rather, they focus on the strengths the child brings to the school environment as well as the supports the child needs in order to build on those strengths.

Teachers are in a position to have a significant impact on the cognitive profile of children living with violence.

Fourteen of 100 children between the ages of 3 and 17 experience family violence.[18] Abuse is one of the environmental factors that influence their emergent metacognitive processes and perceptions of both themselves and the world. The cognitive set these children develop runs counter to some of the assumptions that schools make about how children organize their worlds.

To be successful, to experience competence, these children need classroom teachers who can articulate alternative ways of being and establish a context in which learning can occur. Helping these children learn does not involve moral judgment, but rather requires the specification of thinking about the world. It is a response to a cognitive need, not to a behavioral or a psychiatric one.

Teachers are in a position to have a significant impact on the cognitive profile of children living with violence. Their profession is based on an understanding of how knowledge is constructed and interpreted in everyday behavior. They are skilled at generating functional alternatives and encouraging student individuation, developing student competence, and fostering student control. Their involvement with these children must be clearly articulated and actively sought. For they alone can establish the necessary "goodness of fit" between educational environments and the needs of children who live with violence.

NOTES

1. Harold Martin, "Child Abuse and Child Development," *Child Abuse and Neglect,* vol. 3, 1979, pp. 415–21; and John Money, "Child Abuse: Growth Failure, I.Q. Deficit, and Learning Disability," *Journal of Learning Disabilities,* vol. 120, 1982, pp. 439–46.

2. Jerome Kagan, *The Nature of the Child* (New York: Basic Books, 1984).

3. Susan E. Craig. "The Effect of Parental Aggression on Children's Cognitive Development" (Doctoral dissertation, University of New Hampshire, 1986).

4. Karen Schneider-Rosen and Danie Ciechetti, "The Relationship Between Affect and Cognition in Maltreated Infants: Quality of Attachment and the Development of Visual Self-Recognition," *Child Development,* vol. 55, 1984, pp. 648–58.

5. Elizabeth Elmer, *Children in Jeopardy: A Study of Abused Minors and Their Families* (Pittsburgh: University of Pittsburgh Press, 1967), Paula Kienberger Jaudes and Linda Diamond, "The Handicapped Child and Child Abuse," *Child Abuse and Neglect,* vol. 9, 1985, pp. 341–47; Martin, op. cit.; and Money, op. cit.

6. V. C. Crandell, Walter Katkovsky, and Virginia Crandell, "Children's Beliefs in Their Own Control of Reinforcements in Intellectual-Academic Achievement Situations," *Child Development,* vol. 36, 1965, pp. 91–109.

7. Esther Battle and Julian Rotter, "Children's Feelings of Personal Control as Related to Social Class and Ethnic Group," *Journal of Personality,* vol. 31, 1963, pp. 482–90.

8. Ray E. Helfer and C. Henry Kempe, "Developmental Deficits Which Limit Interpersonal Skills," in idem, eds., *The Battered Child,* 3rd ed. (Chicago: University of Chicago Press, 1980), pp. 36–48.

9. Ibid.

10. Ibid.

11. Martin E. P. Seligman, *Helplessness: On Depression, Development, and Death* (San Francisco: W. H. Freeman, 1975).

12. Linda Anderson, Carolyn Evertson, and Jere Brophy, "An Experimental Study of Effective Teaching in First-Grade Reading Groups," *Elementary School Journal,* vol. 79, 1979, pp. 193–223; Thomas Good and Douglas Grouws, "The Missouri Mathematics Effectiveness Project," *Journal of Educational Psychology,* vol. 71, 1979, pp. 355–62; Madeline Hunter, *Increasing Your Teaching Effectiveness* (Palo Alto, Calif.: Learning Institute,

1981); and Jane Stallings, "How Instructional Processes Relate to Child Outcomes in a National Study of Follow-Through," *Journal of Teacher Education*, Spring 1976, pp. 43–47.

13. John I. Goodlad, *A Place Called School* (New York: McGraw-Hill, 1984); and David Johnson and Roger Johnson, *Learning Together and Alone: Cooperation, Competition, and Individualization* (Englewood Cliffs, N.J.: Prentice-Hall, 1975). See also the special symposium on social interdependence in the classroom, for which Johnson and Johnson served as guest editors, in the fall 1978 issue of *Journal of Research and Development in Education*, pp. 1–152; David Johnson et al., *Circles of Learning: Cooperation in the Classroom* (Alexandria, Va.: Association for Supervision and Curriculum Development, 1984); Bruce Joyce and Maurice Weil, *Models of Teaching*, 2nd ed., (Englewood Cliffs, N.J.: Prentice-Hall, 1980); and Robert E. Slavin, *Cooperative Learning* (New York: Longman, 1983).

14. Hunter, op. cit.

15. Johnson and Johnson, eds., special symposium, and Slavin, op. cit.

16. Karen Harris and Michael Pressley, "The Nature of Cognitive Strategy Instruction: Interactive Strategy Construction," *Exceptional Children*, vol. 57, 1991, pp. 392–406.

17. James C. Chalfant, Margaret V. D. Pysh, and R. Moultrie, "Teacher Assistance Teams: A Model for Within-Building Problem Solving," *Learning Disability Quarterly*, vol. 2, 1979, pp. 85–96.

18. Murray A. Straus and Glenda Kaufman Kantor, "Stress and Child Abuse," in Ray E. Helfer and Ruth S. Kempe, eds., *The Battered Child*, 4th ed. (Chicago: University of Chicago Press, 1988), p. 49.

Research Raises Troubling Questions About Violence Prevention Programs

by Marc Posner

There's no evidence that they reduce serious violence and growing concern that the design of many school-based programs is too simplistic.

It's every principal's nightmare. The sound of gunshots. The phone call imploring you to rush to the cafeteria where an argument that began on the street has exploded. And when the ambulance and the police have gone there will be television cameras, microphones, and reporters' questions, a deluge of phone calls from frightened parents, and an emergency school board meeting. The question you will hear over and over is "What are you going to do to make sure this does not happen again?"

> **Few administrators under pressure to "do something" about violence have the resources or the expertise...**

An increasing number of public and private school administrators face situations involving serious violence perpetrated by and against adolescents. School officials are responding by adding violence prevention programs—often a commercially available "off-the-shelf" package—to their schools' already overcrowded curricula. But few administrators under pressure to "do something" about violence have the resources or the expertise to assess the extent of their school's violence problem, to judge whether the program

From *The Harvard Education Newsletter*, vol. X, no. 3, p. 1–4, May/June 1994. Reprinted with permission.

they have chosen is appropriate for their students, or to find evidence that the program actually works. In fact, researchers are beginning to question whether the most commonly used school-based programs for violence prevention and conflict resolution actually do what they are supposed to do.

MORE HARM THAN GOOD?

Most evaluations of these programs reveal little evidence of success. Daniel Webster of the Injury Prevention Center at Johns Hopkins University reviewed evaluations of three widely used curricula—the Violence Prevention Curriculum for Adolescents by Deborah Prothrow-Stith, the Washington (D.C.) Community Violence Prevention Program, and Positive Adolescent Choices Training—and found "no evidence that such programs produce long-term changes in violent behavior or risk of victimization." Indeed, Webster argues that the main function of these programs is to provide "political cover" for school officials and politicians, and that they may do more harm than good by distracting the public from the real causes of youth violence.

A survey of 51 programs by Renee Wilson-Brewer and colleagues at the Education Development Center (EDC) in Newton, Massachusetts, found that fewer than half even claimed to have reduced levels of violence. Most claimed to have had effects that program staff members assumed would help prevent violence, such as creating community awareness or having a substantial number of students complete the program, but few had any data to back up their assumptions.

Nancy Guerra and Patrick Tolan of the University of Illinois reviewed the existing research and identified some promising strategies warranting further study, but concluded that "well-intentioned efforts are being applied to many children and adolescents without indication of their effects.... Not only have programs that have been earnestly launched been ineffective, but some of our seemingly best ideas have led to worsening the behavior of those subjected to the intervention." This disturbing negative effect, Guerra explains, results from the difficulty of identifying high-risk students. Kids who are wrongly placed in targeted violence prevention programs (which, ironically, seem to have the greatest impact) may become more violence-prone than if they had not been exposed to the programs.

Defenders of the programs blame the lack of evidence of their success on the shortcomings of the evaluations. It is true that few programs have the resources and expertise necessary for evaluating behavioral outcomes and for long-term follow-up. Most evaluations lack adequate sample sizes, matched comparison groups, and objective measures of behavioral outcomes. Many use tests of student attitudes or self-reported behavior that measure little but the students' ability to give the answers expected of them.

> **Well-meaning teachers may "see" a reduction in violence among students where none exists.**

Evaluations based on teachers' classroom observations are equally suspect. Guerra warns that "testimonials should not be confused with evaluations." Well-meaning teachers may "see" a reduction in violence among students where none exists. Or, driven by honest concern and media attention, they may exaggerate the levels of violence that existed before their intervention. Evaluations based on "objective" behavioral outcomes like discipline and arrest records are at the mercy of the inconsistencies of school discipline policies and the juvenile justice system.

FLAWS IN THE DESIGN

Researchers are beginning to suspect that the lack of evidence for success in violence prevention is not just because of inadequate evaluation efforts. Many programs have serious flaws that make them highly unlikely to overcome the inherent difficulties of changing complex human behavior. Too often, they lump together a broad range of behaviors and people, ignoring the fact that different types of people turn to violence for very different reasons.

Few school-based prevention programs target the relatively small group of young people who commit acts of serious violence. Daniel Webster points out that many conflict resolution programs teach the kinds of negotiation skills that may be useful for middle-class students whose disputes stem from competing interests, but not for poor, high-risk youth for whom violence conflict is often a result of macho posturing and competition for status. Nancy Guerra similarly criticizes the notion that a program reflecting middle-class norms will affect the behavior of all violent youth. "A sixteen-year-old who sticks up a McDonald's," she notes, "does not have a conflict with the person behind the cash register."

The field of violence prevention faces an even greater challenge than learning how to target its programs: The inherent difficulty of creating and implementing any school-based program that actually changes behavior. Alcohol and drug-abuse prevention efforts have been subjected to more research, better evaluation, and wider and more consistent implementation than violence prevention programs, yet serious questions remain about the effectiveness of many widely used programs.

> A violence prevention program that takes place over a couple of weeks at one grade level has little hope for success.

This is not to say that alcohol- and drug-abuse prevention efforts never work. Nancy Tobler of the State University of New York examined the evaluations of almost 150 programs and found some that were effective. But the key to success, she says, is knowing "which types of programs should be offered to whom, by whom, and at what age." Programs must take into account the age group being targeted, the drugs being targeted, the selection and training of leaders, and the influence of the community. Many alcohol and drug programs, and most violence prevention programs, ignore these critical variables.

Violence often results from a complex interaction of environmental, social, and psychological factors such as the learned behavior of responding to conflict with violence, the effects of drugs or alcohol, the presence of weapons, the absence of positive family relationships and adult supervision. Few violence prevention programs can muster the resources to affect all the possible causes.

Behavioral skills learned in school health classes and substance-abuse prevention programs generally suffer a marked decline after six months. The key to providing students with the skills, knowledge, and motivation they require to become healthy adults is a comprehensive program that responds to the new risks and pressures that arise with each developmental stage. The onset of puberty, the increased presence of alcohol, drugs, and weapons in a young person's environment, and growing economic pressures all increase the risk of being a perpetrator or a victim of violence. A violence prevention program that takes place over a couple of weeks at one grade level has little hope of success. Addressing these risks requires a sustained effort over the child's entire school career.

PROMISING STRATEGIES

Educators have neither the resources nor the responsibility to change all the social factors that impel young people toward violence. But they do have the power to make some changes in their schools. Children at high risk of violence, academic failure, drug abuse, and dropping out often lack a connection to any positive social entity—family, peer group, or church. Guerra and Tolan found that many of the most promising strategies were family interventions that taught parenting skills and improved family relationships. They also found evidence to suggest that effective school-based programs should focus not just on students but on the school itself as well.

> **...many of the most promising strategies were family interventions that taught parenting skills and improved family relationships.**

Schools that provide a positive social attachment for youth can, at least in part, lessen the estrangement and hopelessness that lead kids to the alternative culture of gangs. Daniel Webster suggests assigning teams of teachers to follow cohorts of students through several grades, instead of changing teachers every year. This, he argues, can create more positive and lasting bonds between students and their school. Webster also suggests keeping schools open for supervised extracurricular activities on afternoons, evenings, and weekends, and during the summer. Keeping students away from the streets, gangs, drugs, and boredom for even a few hours after classes will at least diminish the amount of time that the negative influences have to do their work. At the same time, there is no hard evidence from evaluations that such strategies actually work better than others.

Schools may also have a part to play in protecting students from risks they encounter outside the classroom. Some researchers have attributed the dramatic increase in serious violence among youth to two intersecting trends: a large increase in the population of young men (the group that commits most violent crimes) and the unprecedented availability and acceptability of guns—especially semi-automatic handguns. The presence of a gun can lead to violence in situations where the presence of a different weapon, even a knife, will not. Obviously, a bullet fired in anger can cause more injury than a punch or slap.

> The presence of a gun can lead to violence in situations where the presence of a different weapon, even a knife, will not.

Increased attention is being focused on school-based programs to steer youth away from carrying guns and associating with those who do. While there is no good evidence as yet about how well such programs work, the fact that they require less of a behavioral change on the part of students than some other approaches may be cause for optimism. On the other hand, these gun programs cannot be thought of as a substitute for what has become an almost universally accepted maxim in the public health community—that the most effective intervention for serious violence would be to outlaw the possession, manufacture, and sale of these weapons.

Television, movies, rap music, and video games are frequently criticized for their violent content and its presumed ill effects on young people. Much of this criticism is simplistic and ignores the more complex causes of violence. Still, the research on violence and the media (including that on sexual violence and pornography) indicates that a consistent depiction of violence as an acceptable method of resolving conflicts or increasing status and self-esteem contributes to the forces that impel so many youth toward this behavior. Critical viewing and media literacy programs that teach children how to interpret what they see and hear may be of some help.

LET THE BUYER BEWARE

While violence prevention programs are not *the* solution, carefully designed, targeted, and implemented programs with good teacher training and technical support may be part of the solution. The Tolan-Guerra and EDC reviews suggest that strategies including cognitive mediation programs (in which young people are taught to change those habits of thought that lead them to respond violently to conflict) have shown some success in changing behavior. Webster, however, questions the potential of classroom interventions for changing habits acquired much earlier in life.

Whatever the merits of school-based violence prevention programs, there is no value in implementing the wrong program for the wrong reasons. Administrators should carefully assess their needs before adopting any program. Nancy Guerra reminds school officials that "one incident does not make a problem." One student caught with a gun does not necessarily mean your school needs metal detectors. If half the students are packing weapons, however, metal detectors can help provide a more secure environment.

Ineffective programs can be dangerous if administrators and parents are lulled into thinking they are addressing the problem when they are not.

Guerra also warns administrators to be careful consumers and not just grab the first program that comes across their desks. In many cases, she says, "whatever program has the glossiest cover and the best marketing plan gets implemented." She points out that ineffective programs can be dangerous if administrators and parents are lulled into thinking they are addressing the problem when they are not. Informed choices and effective strategies require input from parents, teachers, law enforcement agencies, and medical, public health, and social service personnel.

A good model at the state level is Illinois, which has amended its School Code to require districts to provide violence prevention or conflict resolution education in grades 4 through 12. As part of the effort, the Illinois Council for the Prevention of Violence has established a curriculum task force including representatives of a wide range of state and local groups. The task force is creating a framework for reviewing violence prevention curricula, identifying gaps, and making recommendations for the use of such curricula in Illinois schools. It will also pilot violence prevention programs in five districts to determine what kinds of technical assistance and other resources are most helpful.

THE POWER OF SOCIAL DECAY

We must also be realistic about the strength of the social forces that impel children towards violence. Even long-term educational interventions are not sufficient for children in neighborhoods whose economies and social structures are in ruins. Thus school health programs are increasingly being supplemented by breakfast and lunch programs and school-based health services. Violence prevention may prove most effective when it is one of a number of services offered as part of a "full-service school."

But violence is not like malnutrition or infectious diseases. Immunization in a school clinic can protect a child from measles. A good school breakfast and lunch can help make up for the lack of any dinner. But a ten-session violence prevention course cannot overcome the deprivations of a life of poverty or the pressures toward violence in the world outside school.

The burden of preventing violence cannot lie solely, or even primarily, on the shoulders of educators. Webster points out that many violence prevention programs assume there is "something wrong with the kids" that we can fix with educational intervention. A truer understanding of what is really wrong can be found in President Lyndon Johnson's address to the nation in July 1967, in the wake of a wave of urban violence:

"The only genuine, long-range solution for what has happened lies in an attack—mounted at every level—upon the conditions that breed despair and violence. All of us know what those conditions are: ignorance, discrimination, slums, poverty, disease, not enough jobs. We should attack these conditions—not because we are frightened by conflict, but because we are fired by conscience. We should attack them because there is simply no other way to achieve a decent and orderly society in America."

Intervention: Crisis, Communication, and Commitment

ection Three offers the reader additional recommendations for instructional activities and suggestions for handling the aftermath of violence. We can no longer ask *if* violence will happen in our school; we can only wonder *when*. Developing awareness programs for teachers and parents and a school and district crisis management plan will help reduce violence and manage devastating consequences when violence occurs. Donna Harrington-Lueker's article, Stephanie Kadel and Joseph Follman, and Carter Burns provide specific steps and strategies to prevent and deal with a crisis. David Frisby, a police official, and Joseph Beckham, a former teacher, discuss general guidelines and appropriate uses of force that educators may use in confrontations.

The articles by Mary Nebgen and Kenneth S. Trump focus on the increasing threat and reality of gang violence. Nebgen looks at one city's efforts to keep its streets safe, while Trump offers practical steps that schools and communities can take to protect against gang involvement.

We need to rethink our methods for handling violent students. Considering alternatives to expulsion and supervision may open new options for educators as well as for students. Current research does not support the belief that harsh punishment will deter violent and aggressive behavior; restoration may be the answer. Solutions will not be found in continuing the treatments of the past nor in any single intervention. We need to have a variety of options that can address the problems in a multitude of ways.

The criminal justice system must form partnerships with schools and other social service agencies to create programs and options that do more than add to the already crowded prisons and correctional institutions. Peter Schmidt, Philip Stelly, and Sara Podell discuss some of the legal issues and problems that arise when dealing with youth and crime. Schmidt discusses the legal repercussions of punishing youngsters who commit a crime, while Stelly discusses the sticky issue of protecting students without infringing on their rights. Podell examines some of the problems in the criminal justice system and offers possible remedies. A final piece by Gus Frias encourages educators and community leaders to work together to develop a national strategy for safe schools.

Can You Protect Kids From Society's Senseless Violence?

by Donna Harrington-Lueker

E verybody's worst nightmare" is what Stockton, Calif., Superintendent Mary Gonzalez Mend called it. Patrick Purdy, a 24-year old drifter dressed in an Army flak jacket and jeans, had strafed a crowded elementary school playground with 105 rounds from an AK-47 assault rifle. Five children died; 30 others, including one teacher, were wounded by blasts so powerful that some bullets sliced completely through school walls and were found later on the front lawn.

Stockton, reeling with shock and grief, saw its tragedy played out on the evening news and in the press, an unrelenting reminder of the grim truth of the '80s. Nowhere is there sanctuary from the random violence of American life. Not even in the school yard.

It is a reality many school executives are only beginning to face.

But face it you must, whether you are a principal on the front lines or a superintendent ministering to school security from the central office. After the events of the last year, you can no longer afford not to plan for the unthinkable. You dare not become complacent about school security in the naive belief that "it can't happen here."

> You dare not become complacent about school security in the naive belief that "it can't happen here."

It can, and it did. On May 20, 1988, eight months before Patrick Purdy opened fire in Stockton, 30-year-old Laurie Dann entered the Hubbard Woods Elementary School in the quiet

From *The Executive Educator,* vol. 11, no. 6, p. 13–16, June 1989. Reprinted with permission.

Chicago suburb of Winnetka and, with a .32-caliber Smith & Wesson and a .22-caliber Beretta, killed one eight-year-old boy and wounded five other children. Fleeing the school after the shooting (a substitute teacher had grabbed Dann's gun hand after refusing to herd her second graders together), Dann holed up in a nearby house, where she took her own life.

Four months later, on September 26, 1988, 19-year-old James William Wilson walked through the front door of the Oakland Elementary School in Greenwood, S.C., pulled a .22-caliber nine-shot revolver from his belt, and opened fire, killing two eight-year-old girls and wounding nine others.

For Winnetka Superintendent Donald Monroe, the lesson of these events was clear. "Stockton and Greenwood, following [our own tragedy] in close succession, exploded the notion that Laurie Dann was a freak accident," the superintendent observes, his tone measured, his words patient and reflective. "We realized we had more cause for concern than we'd originally thought.

"All of us," Monroe adds, "came to the difficult understanding that our schools are just not as safe as we once thought they were."

Complete safety is a memory, but these devices can increase school security

If you think you can buy complete school security, think again. The high-tech monitoring devices you depend on to protect your school against nighttime vandals or daytime computer thieves won't be much help when you're trying to protect personnel rather than property.

But some hardware has its place as part of a total security program, most school safety experts agree. Larry Burgan, chief of police for the Baltimore City Schools, is one of them. On the basis of his 22 years of experienced in the security business, Burgan offers this lowdown on school security equipment:

   • **Door and window locks.** Burgan speaks highly of the lowly door lock. "Our policy here is that all exterior doors . . . are locked from the outside except for an unidentifiable entrance door that's closest to the main office," Burgan says. (The doors, by law, are also equipped with panic bars that allow them to be opened from the inside only.

Locks don't have to be expensive, Burgan says: What you want is a good, simple mechanical device with panic hardware that will keep things secure "under ordinary circumstances." Sure, locked doors will yield to a determined intruder with a crowbar—but not without making a racket someone will hear and attend to.

Whatever locks you buy, though, they'll be only as good as your staff's resolve to keep the doors locked. Burgan advised regular door checks throughout the day as part of any security plan.

As for window locks, he maintains, they're more pertinent to after-hours security than to daytime vigilance. The exception: "If a classroom is vacant, then it's important to have windows down and secure."

• **Door buzzers.** If you want to secure your front door as well, door buzzers (much like home doorbells) might be the answer. Some of Baltimore City's elementary schools have buzzers, which Burgan says can be effective "if they're used properly." In other words, once you install the buzzer, you have to make sure it's staff members who respond to it. "You can't just say to some nine-year-old, 'go open the door, please.'"

The hardware itself is cheap (approximately $20), Burgan notes, and so is installation. Many schools, he points out, have their own electricians.

But buzzers aren't common and probably aren't needed in schools in which the front office has a clear view of the entranceway and an adult is checking visitors in.

• **Video monitors.** "Surely you jest," says a skeptical Burgan. "Monitors at an entrance area just aren't a sensible solution." For one thing, someone has to watch the screens all day, every day to spot trouble and deal with it. For another, the video monitors that work so well in banks and department stores aren't much help spotting the one person who doesn't belong in the jostling crowds of students coming in and out six and seven times a day.

Burgan lobbies instead for "on-site adult presence" during the hectic hours of arrival and departure, an aide at the desk to sign visitors in, and a firm commitment to keeping your perimeter doors locked. "If you put a television at the front door and think you've kept everybody out," he concludes, "you're only kidding yourself."

• **Card-access machines.** You've seen them—one locked door, one plastic card electronically encoded with an open-sesame number, and one handy machine to read the number and open the door. In isolated cases (controlling access to the school's computer room or the staff parking lot, for example), these devices can be effective. Burgan says. But they're expensive. And the more students and teachers need to keep track of, the less feasible it is to use card-access machines.

- **Two-way intercoms.** "Every school should have one in every classroom," Burgan says unequivocally. Install the intercom where it's easily accessible (ideally, teachers shouldn't have to leave their desks to activate the intercom), and look for a model that gives the teacher some way to let the main office know there is a problem without having to say a word. (In some systems, the teacher can flip a switch and trigger a light on a control panel down the hall in the office.)

- **Panic buttons.** These minitransmitters operate on a simple principle: Press the button, the front office or school security is alerted to the fact that you're in trouble, and help comes running. Typically, the transmitters are either hand-held or wall-mounted. Burgan doesn't recommend hand-carried panic buttons, though, largely because of the number of false alarms they're likely to deliver. (People forget they have them and accidentally press the button, he notes.) As for wall-switch models, he says they're better if they're included as part of an intercom system.

- **Two-way radios.** Burgan (and other security experts) can't say enough about keeping in touch with the main office, and for teachers at "remote locations" (loading buses or supervising the playground, for example), this often means carrying a two-way radio. Two-way radios are effective, comparatively cheap, and typically do not have to be licensed for school-based communication. (Radios with super-strong signals might require a Federal Communications Commission permit.) Burgan's officers carry $12,000 models with long-life batteries and an expensive system of satellite receivers. But in most cases, he says, schools can buy "something completely adequate" for less than $300.

Whatever you do, Burgan cautions, recognize that any hardware is only as good as the people who use it. "People fail more than the mechanical stuff does," he concludes. His advice? Go ahead and install security devices—but don't relax your vigilance once the equipment is in place.—D.H.L.

NO MATCH FOR AN AK-47

But if schools aren't safe, what can you do to protect your students and staff against the threat of an armed intruder? There are no sure answers, as some school people learned this past year as they scrambled to meet the threat that suddenly seemed to loom outside the schoolhouse walls.

The options varied. In Washington, D.C., for example, where a young gunman wounded four high school students only days after the Stockton assault, school board members discussed requiring students to wear school uniforms as a security measure. (Uniforms, the reasoning went, would make a stranger easier to spot.)

In Omaha, school system employees were taught hand signals and code words so that, if the occasion arose, they could unobtrusively tell one another to call the police. And in Mentor, Ohio, students practice scrambling under their desks for protection when teachers called out "Earthquake drill!" Building-jarring quakes, though, were far from the teachers' minds: Instead, the drill was designed to get students under their desks (without upsetting them) in case an armed intruder entered the school.

> If you're really going to secure a school then it's not called school. It's called prison.

But as school safety experts will tell you, code words and uniforms are no match for a lunatic with a gun in his hand. "Is an aide going to say at the front door when someone walks up with an AK-47?" asks Robert Rubel, director of the National Alliance for Safe Schools in Bethesda, Md.

"Face it," says Ronald Stephens, executive director of the National School Safety Center in Encino, Calif., realistically stating the obvious: "It's difficult to stop a mentally deranged person with a semiautomatic weapon bent on causing damage in an open place."

And until recently, schools have prided themselves on being open, accessible, public places: parents, teachers, and community members, in fact, have come to expect that accessibility. High walls, concertina wire, armed guards, and cement barricades haven't been part of the schools' profile.

Rubel puts the problem succinctly: "If you're really going to secure a school," says the safety consultant, "then it's not called school. It's called prison."

Instead, safety consultants like Rubel advise school executives to take a critical look at what schools in Greenwood and Winnetka are doing today as they work to develop a total school security plan.

In the aftermath of the Winnetka shooting, schools there have adopted a number of security measures.

- All doors except the front door are kept locked, and every visitor is greeted at the front door by PTA volunteers, who ask them to sign in and wear a name tag. "It's a friendly greeting," explains Superintendent Donald Monroe. But the sign-in procedure serves its purpose: It helps heighten staff awareness of strangers. "If there's someone who's a stranger to us, someone without a name tag," Monroe explains, "we know it's cause to be concerned, to say, 'Can I help you?'"

> **Schools absolutely have to have teacher-initiated two-way communications.**

- School officials installed windows in two Winnetka schools to allow people in the school office to keep close tabs on who comes and goes. In one case, officials replaced an entire wall with a bank of windows to improve visibility.
- The main office of each Winnetka school now has an emergency button: When the button sounds, the police roll immediately. "It might just save a minute or a half-minute" over the typical practice of dialing 911, Monroe explains. "But those seconds could count." After pressing the emergency button, school officials plan to follow up with a 911 call to let police officers know what they'll face when they arrive.
- Intercoms are being installed in every classroom.
- Each elementary school now has a full-time nurse. Before the shooting, nurses in the 1,500-student district worked half-time; the day of the shooting, Monroe observes, the school was fortunate: The half-time Hubbard Woods nurse was on duty, and her presence "made a difference."

After the Stockton shooting, Winnetka school officials made another change: The school system's recess policy has been revised so that fewer students take recess at the same time. And when they do, more adults are there to supervise them.

In Greenwood, the unthinkable also has prompted tighter new security measures. Greenwood Superintendent Robert Watson insists, for instance, that schools "absolutely have to have teacher-initiated two-way communications"—that is, an intercom system teachers can use to talk to the main office. In the typical school, Watson notes, such communication is one-way: The principal can talk to each classroom, but teachers can't talk back or initiate a conversation.

A two-way system "probably would have helped immensely" in Greenwood's case, Watson observes. As of this past spring, a PTA group had purchased such a system for one school, and each school had money in its budget for similar purchases.

In addition, Watson reports, most of the outside doors in Greenwood schools now are kept locked, and all visitors enter through a single front door, where school volunteers direct them to the front office. This traffic-control measure increases the chance that any intruder will be spotted quickly, Watson says: "The earlier you know, the quicker you can address" the situation.

> For starters, Rubel and Stephens agree, schools should take a critical look at access—which, as Stephens puts it, you want to control, not prevent.

"Today," Watson maintains, a gunman "wouldn't even get beyond the front door." Last fall, one entered unchallenged.

DESIGNING YOUR SECURITY PLAN

What the Winnetka and Greenwood approaches do is strike a middle ground between resignation ("You can't stop random violence, so why try?") and paranoia ("Let's barricade the school yard")—all the while recognizing that in most schools, the greatest threat comes from day-to-day events inside and not from outside intruders.

And that middle ground is just where the experts advise you to position your schools' security plan. For starters, Rubel and Stephens agree, schools should take a critical look at access— which, as Stephens puts it, you want to control, not prevent. That means closing off some entrances (usually all but the front door), posting notices that all visitors should report to the front office, and having all visitors sign in. (Adequate signage, telling how to find the front door and the front office, becomes more important when other access is shut off.)

If your school is serious about security, adds Rubel, you will also insist on issuing badges that are numbered and cross-referenced with the names in the visitor's log. That way, he explains, people are less likely to walk off with badges and return later on their own. If the badges are large or brightly colored, and if staff members are trained to be vigilant, badges also can be a practical way to keep tabs on who belongs and who doesn't.

A school that's serious about security also will make certain the main office has a clear view of the front door, something that is "frequently not the case," says Rubel. "What you want is actually to see who goes right or left at Main Street." His message: vigilance.

Finally, as part of access control, both these security experts urge schools to increase adult supervision—whether it's parents patrolling the hallways, custodians checking to see if doors are locked after recess, or volunteers working the registration desk.

> If the [intruder] feels at high risk, he'll avoid the situation. If the risk is low, he simply might not.

Will badges and volunteers stop a determined intruder? Probably not, the experts agree. But as part of an ongoing security strategy, such practices can heighten the risk to intruders. "If the [intruder] feels at high risk, he'll avoid the situation," observes Timothy Crowe, director of the National Crime Prevention Institute at the University of Louisville. "If the risk is low, he simply might not."

The second important part of any school security plan, these experts say, is communication: If something does happen, you need to know about it right away—as do the police and other staff members.

"Your people have to be able to call for assistance from a remote location," notes the National School Safety Center's Stephens, who advises using walkie-talkies or other two-way radios while supervising the playground, loading buses, or conducting perimeter checks. Inside the school, Stephens advises "something more than a panic button," which simply signals that someone's in trouble. More useful, he says, are systems that allow two-way conversation.

The third major consideration for the security-conscious school is developing its own crisis plan. "How will teachers control and monitor children during a crisis?" asks Stephens by way of example. "Where will they move them if they have to? Does the school have evacuation plans?"

"Schools should have plans in place for fleeing the scene, evacuating a building, and even closing down and sealing off an area," adds Timothy Crowe.

Greenwood's Watson allows that his schools didn't have such a plan last fall, and many children "ran into the woods in a blind panic" after their teachers evacuated them through the school windows. The result: chaos. Today, Greenwood has a plan that involves keeping students together after they're evacuated and moving them to specific areas where they have a better chance of being safe.

TAKING THE LONG VIEW

If all this sounds just a little bit nebulous, it's because, quite simply, there are no easy answers. A security program that might be appropriate for an inner-city school with a high crime rate and rampant discipline problems might be overkill for a tiny school in a quiet suburb where the crime rate hovers near zero and shows no signs of climbing. ("Are we talking Detroit or Tinley Park?" Rubel asks with a hint of exasperation when pressed repeatedly for some hard-and-fast security rules.) Programs have to be tailored to fit specific situations and then diligently followed without exception.

> In many cases, older schools didn't put a premium on good visual access, traffic control, or the need for inside, natural surveillance.

Effective programs, in fact, avoid what Crowe calls "the knee-jerk reaction" in which "a school system without an administrative commitment to security decides that it just needs something for this terrorist action." What schools actually need is a total security presence, he says, and that's something few U.S. school systems have. "The key," says Crowe, "is integrating security into how you run your system."

In the long run, too, school systems might profitably look at the way their buildings are designed. One proponent of safety-by-design is Greenwood's Robert Watson, who has spoken throughout the South about the lessons his school system learned from last fall's shooting.

"When many schools were designed," he says, "safety was different" and schools were content if they could keep out nighttime vandals. The result: In many cases, older schools didn't put a premium on good visual access, traffic control, or the need for inside, natural surveillance—all of which safety experts are emphasizing today.

> School security takes cooperation and interest and concern on a continuing basis from everyone in the school.

A junior high school in his own district has what Watson considers a promising design: Hallways emanate from a central office area like spokes from a wheel. Standing at the hub, Watson says, the principal can see virtually everything at a glance; he is in control.

Schools also need to create a sense of ownership, adds Timothy Crowe, who advocates security through environmental design. Crowe's principle is a simple one: In a good security program, physical spaces are organized in such a way as to encourage people to be observant, to notice what's going on (including the arrival of strangers).

And in this respect, says Crowe, traditional school design ("the kind that was popular 20 or 30 years ago") just might have an edge over the multipurpose approach favored in the '60s and '70s. "In the traditional approach, all spaces were typically assigned to somebody," explains Crowe. "Everybody had their own turf," and their "proprietal concern" translated into increased awareness and vigilance.

In many newer buildings, though, the space belongs to everyone—and no one. People come and go, and teachers are typically grouped in an office ("the bull-pen approach," says Crowe) rather than having their own rooms. Proprietary concern in such buildings is nominal.

School architects, skeptical about the value of adopting a bunker-mentality, deliver a similar message: Often, it's the subtle approach that best balances a school's need to provide security with its need to preserve a proper learning environment. For John Castellana, chairman of the American Institute of Architects' national committee for school design, that means reducing the number of exterior entrances and increasing visibility. Castellana also favors play areas adjacent to classrooms ("for direct accessibility") with a little "creative screening and walling" to give teachers and staff a sense of security without reducing visibility. "Play areas and exterior spaces need to be semi-controlled and observable in an instant," says Castellana, who adds that he's currently designing an elementary school that will have emergency telephones on the playground.

In the long term, though, there's no substitute for vigilance. "What's safe is usually not what's convenient," notes Larry Burgan, chief of police for the Baltimore City Schools and a school safety consultant for the U.S. Justice Department. "You have to be on top of things every day.

"School security takes cooperation and interest and concern on a continuing basis from everyone in the school."

Put another way, good school security is what protects students long after the media spotlight fades.

Crisis Management and Response

by Stephanie Kadel and Joseph Follman

A clear, well-organized plan may mean the difference between level-headed actions and solutions or danger and panic.
S. Greenbaum, B. Gonzalez, & N. Ackley, *Educated Public Relations: School Safety 101*, 1989

How can a school prepare for and respond to a crisis? Violent incidents can range from a fight between two students to a major crisis such as a slaying by an armed intruder. While the latter crisis may seem a remote possibility to many administrators, such incidents can occur anywhere. Therefore, a school must be prepared for the worst. Schools that are prepared for major crises will also be better able to handle more common disruptions and other crises such as suicide and accidental death of a student.

1. CREATING A CRISIS MANAGEMENT PLAN

Every school should design its own plan of action for a crisis. District administrators may want to supply principals with general suggestions for procedures, but plans must be tailored to a school's available staff, building design, and other factors. The most effective plans are designed by a team from the school—including teachers, administrators, students, counselors, bus drivers, security personnel, and other staff—as well as representatives from the school district office, law enforcement, and health services. Ciminillo (1980) recommends designating such a group as the "school safety committee" and asking them

From *Hot Topics: Usable Research, Reducing School Violence*, the SouthEastern Regional Vision for Education, 1993, p. 3–17. Reprinted with permission.

to be responsible not only for developing a crisis management plan but for recommending strategies to create a safer school environment.

In preparing for a violent incident, the school safety committee should identify all necessary tasks for handling the incident and assign staff members—and back-ups—to be responsible for each task. Such tasks may include the following:

- informing the district office,
- accompanying injured students to hospitals,
- maintaining order and calm on the campus,
- coordinating transportation,
- coordinating communication among the school, parents, and the media,
- identifying injured or killed students and adults, and
- notifying parents and spouses

(National School Safety Center [NSSC], 1990a).

> **A list of who is responsible for what during a crisis and important telephone numbers should be posted in the school office and given to staff.**

The committee should take into consideration all possible crises when deciding what tasks may need to be addressed. The principal will most likely assume authority in a crisis situation, but someone should be designated to fill this role in the principal's absence. All staff should be informed of this chain of authority (Ciminillo, 1980).

Once a crisis management plan is developed, school staff (all full-time and part-time employees including bus drivers and substitute teachers) should be given training in the procedures and their responsibilities. Training in and practice of the crisis management plan are especially important because people can panic in an emergency. This training should include information on how to recognize and anticipate violent incidents and how to report an incident to the main office. Students should be taught crisis management and have an opportunity to practice emergency procedures. For example, schools can hold drills during which teachers secure all doors and windows and keep all students in the classroom (Speck, 1992). Any crisis management plan should be reviewed and updated periodically to train new staff and reflect changes in school, district, law enforcement, and media procedures. A list of who is responsible for what during a crisis and important telephone numbers should be posted in the school office and given to staff. A copy of this list should also be sent to the district office.

Guidelines for responding to a violent incident (Table 1) have been compiled from the plans of a number of school districts. They are presented in a specified order, but each incident requires its own priorities, and tasks can happen simultaneously as various staff members take on their assigned roles. School safety committees may find these suggestions helpful in designing their own procedures.

Table 1
Responding to a Violent Incident

- Assess the situation. How serious is it? What elements of the school's crisis management plan are relevant? Assemble all necessary school staff members.
- Depending on the incident, either defuse the situation or call in school security and/or police officers for assistance. If long-term involvement of law enforcement is necessary, provide space and equipment for a "command post."
- Alert all school staff to the situation and let teachers know what they should do with their classes, e.g., lock classroom doors or leave the building. Also, make sure that teachers account for all their students.
- Separate victims from perpetrators as quickly as possible and attempt to identify all those involved.
- Call for medical assistance if necessary and assign a staff person to the hospital where students are to be taken.
- Assign a staff member to remain with victims while medical and/or emotional assistance is being obtained.
- Inform the appropriate school district official of the situation; he or she should notify relevant district personnel and other schools in the area if necessary.
- Record the names of witnesses and encourage them to cooperate with the investigation if one is necessary.
- Disperse onlookers and update students and staff on the situation as soon as possible.
- Notify parents of involved students and spouses of involved school employees if appropriate.

- Prepare to communicate with other parents, concerned community members, and the media.
- Develop and follow procedures for reuniting parents with their children in the event of a severe crisis.
- Develop and follow procedures for withdrawing security and/or law enforcement personnel after the incident is over.
- Prepare a detailed report of the incident for school and district records.

(Blauvelt, 1981; Blount, 1986; Dade County Public Schools, 1988; Fulton County School System, 1991; Gaustad, 1991)

While a severe crisis such as a homicide or hostage-taking requires immediate intervention by law enforcement, other violent incidents, such as fights or suspected weapons possessions, may be defused without the help of police. Police should be notified afterward, however, if the incident is a criminal act. The school safety committee will have to decide on proper procedures for handling such incidents. Some procedures for responding to student fighting are listed in Table 2.

Table 2
Procedures for Stopping a Fight

- If a teacher in a classroom is informed that there is a fight, he or she should send a reliable student to the office to summon assistance.
- When in sight of the altercation, speak loudly and let everyone know that the behavior should stop immediately.
- If possible, obtain help from other teachers.
- Call out to any of the students you recognize and start giving orders. Attempt to get students away from the commotion as quickly as possible.
- If you know the fighting students by name, call out each of their names and let them know they have been identified.
- If confronted with a serious fight, especially one that involves weapons, get additional help; do not try to be a hero.
- After separating the students, try to avoid using further confrontational behavior yourself (i.e., do not point at the students, make accusations, or corner them with their backs against the wall).

> • Remember that no one can "cool down" instantly; give the
> students time to talk in a calm setting and gradually change
> the climate of the situation.
> (Blauvelt, 1981; Greenbaum, Turner, & Stephens, 1989)

If a weapon has been reported in someone's possession or
somewhere in the school, administrators can alert custodial
staff to check various "hiding places" in and around the school
building and assign staff to remain highly visible until the
weapon is found (Blauvelt, 1981). Searches of suspected students' lockers and/or belongings are also allowable if there are
reasonable grounds for suspicion (Rapp, Carrington, &
Nicholson, 1992). Any weapons that are found should be
turned over to the police, not kept in the school (Blauvelt,
1981).

2. ESTABLISHING COMMUNICATION

Fast and effective communication among school personnel can
be critical during a crisis. An intercom system linked to all classrooms is probably the most common means of communication
during an emergency. While intercoms are standard in most
schools today, teachers who are located in portable buildings or
whose classes are held outside should be contacted personally.
To avoid unnecessarily alarming the students, teachers and administrators should agree on a code phrase, to be announced
over the intercom, to signal that teachers should take emergency precautions. Walkie-talkies and a bullhorn may also be
useful communication tools (Gaustad, 1991).

Students

Sharing the facts with students is especially important during a
crisis in order to keep them calm and to discourage rumors
(Fulton County School System, 1991). Students should be
regularly updated on events and given clear instructions on
what to do until the crisis is over. Depending on the circumstances, it may not be appropriate or ethical to divulge the
names of students or staff involved in the crisis, but students
should be informed about what the school is doing to respond
to the situation.

Faculty and Staff

Since teachers are the most direct link to students, it is vital that they know what is happening. If they all have the same information, they can reassure students and squelch unfounded student rumors. Therefore, an early morning or afternoon faculty meeting should be held in the immediate aftermath of a crisis to bring teachers and staff up-to-date on what has happened and how the school has responded. This meeting should include the principal and perhaps the district superintendent. If it is not possible to arrange such a meeting, a memo may be circulated to all teachers and staff members that describes what has occurred and how the school has responded thus far.

> **Teachers are the most direct link to students. It is vital that they be kept informed in the event of a crisis.**

Parents

Schools should establish procedures for communicating with parents during and after a crisis. No matter what the incident, the parents of students who were involved in a crisis must be contacted immediately. Depending on the severity of the situation, school and district staff may be enlisted to contact all parents individually to pick up their children at school. Another option is to dismiss students in the usual manner, using buses for transportation, and to send home a written statement which explains the events that took place at school and the actions taken. Once word gets out to parents and other concerned community residents, they will seek additional information by calling the school or district offices. Staff receiving such calls need a written statement of information to share and should practice handling such calls (Fulton County School System, 1991).

Outside Resources

Proper communication is also important with intervention agencies and services such as law enforcement, hospitals and medical emergency services, mental health and social services, and other community support groups. The school safety committee should contact these services in advance of a crisis to verify the correct phone number, appropriate contact person, and proper procedures to take in an emergency (Gaustad, 1991). A list of intervention services should be posted in the main office. The National School Safety Center (1990a) further recommends keeping an unlisted telephone line available at all times for official use and a portable telephone in the office in case phone lines are disabled.

3. WORKING WITH THE MEDIA

The school safety committee should assign at least one staff person to work with the media during a serious crisis. The principal or district-level administrator may act as the official spokesperson for the school in a crisis situation, but another staff member can assume responsibility for organizing the details. In preparation for dealing with the media, this person should become familiar with the reporter and editor who typically cover school news or who receive news releases from the school district (Greenbaum, Gonzalez, & Ackley, 1989). Staff should act as "media lookouts" during a crisis in order to greet reporters and direct them to the school's official spokesperson (Fulton County School System, 1991). If a news conference will be held, reporters can be taken directly to a designated room (see Table 3). The school's representative can also learn how the media may be of help to the school (by publicizing an information hot line number, for example).

Table 3
Working with Media During a Crisis:
Tips for the School Spokesperson

- Ensure all media inquiries are routed to one person or office.
- Prepare an official statement about the particular crisis and action being taken. Include information to answer basic who, what, when, where, why, and how questions, but do not reveal names of students or employees involved in the incident. Read from or distribute this statement when media inquiries are made. This same statement should be shared with teachers, staff, and students to ensure that they are given accurate, consistent information.
- Be brief. Avoid providing superfluous information or using professional jargon.

- Anticipate media questions, especially for potentially controversial issues.
- Answer one question at a time, and answer only the question that is asked.
- As official spokesperson, do not hesitate to say, "I don't know" or "I will have to get back with you" to a reporter's question. A reply of "no comment" suggests that information is being withheld. Remember to follow up when information is available; bear in mind that the public has a right to know and to understand what has happened.
- Try not to appear to be concerned mainly about the school's reputation.
- Ignore abrasive comments made by reporters and maintain a professional attitude.
- Do not treat anything as "off the record."
- Provide updates to the media as events unfold, even after the initial crisis is handled.
- Keep calm. Show sensitivity to the seriousness of the matter, but do not overreact.

(Fulton County School System, 1991; Gaustad, 1991; Greenbaum, Gonzalez, & Ackley, 1989; NSSC, 1990a)

4. AIDING VICTIM RECOVERY

All school staff should be educated about the emotional needs of victims of violence. Gaustad (1991) warns, "Insensitive and unsympathetic reactions by administrators and coworkers can compound the emotional trauma of the attack and lengthen the recovery process" (p. 40). Asking them to fill out confusing forms, wait in an office alone, or meet with the perpetrator can heighten their sense of fear and make them feel doubly victimized. As suggested in the crisis management plan, a staff member should be assigned to attend to victims during a crisis; this person may also help victims obtain the support services that they need.

It is particularly important that the school assign an advocate for the victim(s) of sexual assault. The victim advocate should be of the same sex as the victim, be able to explain to the victim his or her rights, and assist the victim through administrative and criminal proceedings. In addition, the school district should provide written guidelines and information to victims regarding the reporting of crimes, available medical and psychological services, victim rights, and the procedures for dealing with the violation (*Guidelines for Policies Addressing Sexual Misconduct Toward Students in Public Schools*, 1992).

While the primary victims of school violence should rightly receive the most immediate attention to their physical and emotional needs, victims of violence encompass many more people than those who are actually injured or involved in an incident. Witnesses to the event as well as parents, spouses, friends, and teachers of injured or killed students and staff are also affected. While a school cannot be expected to provide long-term individual counseling to all those who may need it, resuming normal functioning after a crisis may require that medical, psychological, and nurturing services be available to students, faculty, and staff. Such services not only assist in the recovery process, but they help prevent angry students from retaliating with further violence (Centers for Disease Control, 1992; Gaustad, 1991).

Mental health experts recommend that school administrators "take a long-term view of dealing with a crisis" because psychological symptoms resulting from a traumatic event may not surface until weeks or months after the incident (NSSC, 1990a, p.16). As part of the crisis management plan, the school safety committee should, therefore, identify mental health professionals who can be called during and after a crisis to work with students, parents, and school staff. The district may also want to establish a team of professionals who can be convened and sent to any school in the district to help with crisis recovery (NSSC, 1990c). Many schools that have been through a traumatic crisis found it beneficial to reopen the day after the crisis, even on weekends, and provide counseling and information for several days. Schools may want to provide ongoing counseling sessions for students.

Because the trauma of witnesses to a violent act can interfere with the grief process, student bystanders should be encouraged to talk about their feelings of loss and their thoughts about anger, injury, racial issues, and/or death. Other students are often confused and frightened after a crisis as well, and they may depend on adults to help them cope with their feelings about the incident and understand why it occurred. Teachers should, therefore, encourage discussions during class about students' feelings of sadness or anger. They should also monitor students' behavior and refer especially troubled students to counselors (Gaustad, 1991).

School faculty and staff may experience delayed psychological effects of their own when the crisis is over. Their needs should be anticipated and support services provided at this time. Childrens' reactions are often influenced by those of teachers and other adults, so it is especially important that faculty and staff receive the counseling they need to more effectively help students.

> Teachers should, therefore, encourage discussions during class about students' feelings of sadness or anger.

When teachers are victimized, they may require special counseling to avoid blaming themselves or viewing the incident as a professional failure. Because an attack on one teacher can erode the sense of security of others, a teacher's coworkers may also need to be reassured of the safety of the school/classroom. In extreme cases, district officials may be asked to transfer some teachers to new schools or work settings or retrain staff members who wish to change jobs (NSSC, 1990a). Assistance with legal, medical, workers' compensation, and other post-incident procedures is usually well-received by victims (Gaustad, 1991).

In addition to community-based support services, administrators across the country who have experienced one of the most severe crises possible—deaths caused by an armed intruder—have developed an informal network to help one another cope and to provide emergency consulting whenever such an event happens elsewhere. While such attacks are rare, they can happen at any school.

5. REPORTING VIOLENT INCIDENTS

The final step in a crisis management plan is to prepare a detailed report of the violent incident for school and district files. The use of incident reports is becoming more and more common; in fact, South Carolina recently passed a law requiring schools to report every crime committed on campus. Some teachers and administrators downplay incidents of violence in their schools; they may wish to avoid bad publicity, being blamed or possibly sued, suffering retaliation from the offender, or having the incident blown out of proportion. Incidents may go unreported because administrators feel the incidents do not represent a serious problem, prefer to rely on their own security and discipline, or suspect the police and courts will not be particularly helpful (Rapp et al., 1992). However, acknowledging crime and reporting it accurately are crucial to understanding the extent of the problem and what is required to address it.

> School systems that do not report existing dangers place both students and staff at risk by giving them a false sense of security.—J. Gaustad, *Schools Respond to Gangs and Violence,* 1991

An effective incident reporting form is designed to ask for answers to the following questions:

- What happened?
- Why did it happen?
- When did it happen?
- Where did it happen?
- Who was involved?
- How did you respond to the complaint?

(Blauvelt, 1981, p. 2)

When developing or implementing an incident reporting system, administrators should consider the following issues:

- How will reports be filed?
- Who will see these reports outside of the school?
- Should someone be assigned to review each report before it is filed?
- Will weekly or monthly summary reports be prepared? If so, who will receive these reports and how will the information be used?
- Who will analyze data from the reports on a regular basis and how will this information be disseminated and used?

(Blauvelt, 1992)

In districts where gangs are a serious problem, a specialized incident reporting system can focus on the gang influence in schools. Portland, Oregon's computerized gang tracking system, for example, provides information on gang members' real names and nicknames, associates, vehicles, weapons, gang-associated clothing, colors, insignia, criminal activities, and more. Such information is available only to school administrators and law enforcement officials (Prophet, 1990).

Incident reporting can answer many of the following questions:

- What kinds of crimes are reported and in what frequency?
- Where and when do crimes occur on campus?
- What types of persons commit school crimes?
- What are the characteristics of the students who are chronic offenders?
- What types of persons are the most likely victims of school crime?
- Is campus crime a reflection of gang activity?

(California State DOE, 1989, p. 21)

With answers to these kinds of questions, schools seeking to improve safety can make informed decisions about what needs to be changed.

6. ENFORCING THE CONDUCT CODE

When a student violates the conduct code, schools must apply appropriate disciplinary strategies. In the event of a serious act of violence, a student must also face criminal charges, but in most cases the school has to decide on the consequences for the offense. When planning a discipline strategy for a violent student, be sure to review the student's record and/or meet with the youth's family to obtain medical, psychological, and social background information. The following subsection discusses the advantages, disadvantages, and limitations of a number of discipline options that schools have used with violent students.

Removing the Student—Dealing with Serious Violent Incidents

• *Out-of-School Suspension.* Schools have a right and a responsibility to remove students whose behavior presents a danger to others. Out-of-school suspension (OSS) is a common form of discipline because it removes the violent student from the school, is easy to administer, requires little planning or resources, and can be applied for a number of infractions (U.S. Department of Justice, 1986). There is no question that OSS is the appropriate school response to many serious violent incidents. But while OSS is sometimes a **necessary** solution, other times it is more of a **convenient** solution. Furthermore, the school's **solution** may create a larger community problem by placing dangerous kids on the streets. In addition, OSS has little chance of preventing future problems at the school if it is not coupled with long-term preventive and rehabilitative strategies.

> **Schools have a right and a responsibility to remove students whose behavior presents a danger to others.**

District and state records indicate that the number of suspensions varies greatly among schools and districts. This disparity exists even among schools and/or districts with similar socioeconomic populations, suggesting that some places are better than others at devising alternatives to OSS. Research has shown that OSS has no demonstrated positive effect on disruptive behavior (Comerford & Jacobson, 1987), and Wheelock (1986) charges that suspension is perhaps the most powerful message of rejection there is in contributing to student disengagement from school. Other disadvantages of OSS are as follows:

• Suspended students are often the most in need of direct instruction and often fail required courses as a result of being suspended.

• High school dropouts are twice as likely to have been suspended as non-dropouts (most prisoners are dropouts—keeping someone in prison costs many times more than keeping him or her in school, even in special programs).

• Suspended students may regard suspension as a vacation or reward.

• Removing students from schools may contribute to delinquency, as many suspended students are left unsupervised.

• Minority students are suspended or expelled in disproportionately high numbers.

(Hodgkinson, 1993; Silva, 1992; Task Force on School Discipline, 1990; U. S. Department of Justice, 1986; Wehlage & Rutter, 1986)

See Table 4 for lists of strategies for reducing expulsions and out-of-school suspensions, particularly for at-risk or disadvantaged students.

• *In-School Suspension.* In-School Suspension (ISS) temporarily relieves the teacher of disruption and denies the student participation in extracurricular activities. ISS also enables the school to offer students services, such as academic tutoring and personal or group counseling, that may help prevent future problems (NSSC, 1990a). After-school detention and Saturday school, variations on ISS, have similar effects. ISS has become popular with many schools. Somewhat surprisingly, however, ISS has not become a replacement for out-of-school suspension, according to the Florida Task Force on School Discipline. Instead, in many schools, "in-school suspension is often used instead of other in-school interventions like corporal punishment, after-school detention, and parent conferences, and not as an alternative to OSS" (Task Force on School Discipline, 1990, p. 45).

Table 4
Suggestions for Reducing Suspensions and Expulsions, Particularly for Disadvantaged Students

- Encourage teachers and administrators to get to know the communities from which their students come and recognize the cultural values that students bring to school. Where possible, involve parents as partners in reducing violent behavior.
- Schools or districts with disproportionately high suspension rates for minority students must recognize that there is a problem. Plans and goals for addressing this disparity should be **written** into school and district plans to reduce violence.
- In interpreting the severity of a student's offense (finding out what happened, who was responsible, what the response will be, whether or not the student can be believed), consistency is paramount.
- The fallacy that students' behavior can be connected to the color of their skin must be discarded. A correlation of students who are suspended or expelled with those who qualify for free or reduced lunch will likely show that socioeconomic level is a far greater predictor of student trouble than race.

- Do not equate being "strict" with dealing with the overall problem of student violence; focus more effort on prevention than on punishment.
- Train administrators and teachers in school and classroom management. Instruction should cover such topics as handling a violent incident, conflict resolution, and crowd control.
- Make every effort to have the staff and administrators of the school match the diversity of the student body. Minority students need role models at all levels in the school.
- Ensure that the school safety committee (or the authors of the school's code of conduct) reflects the cultural diversity of the school. Teachers and an ethnically representative group of students should have a substantive voice in developing conduct codes.
- Educate administrators and teachers to better appreciate the cultures of their students. This training should focus on specific cultures represented in the school and *not* just address the general category of multicultural education.
- Keep in mind the fundamental rule that students who are engaged in work that interests them are far less likely to get into trouble than those who are bored or distracted.
- Institute violence prevention programs for students that are culturally and developmentally appropriate. These programs should acknowledge the violence, racism, and "classism" that many students experience, be designed for different stages of adolescent development, and feature peer instruction and counseling.
- Make violence prevention programs interdisciplinary and multi-institutional.

If ISS is to truly serve as a replacement to sending students home, then planning, counseling, consistency, positive reinforcement, rehabilitation, and follow-up must be included. Incorporating such features, ISS can serve as alternative to out-of-school suspension or to corporal punishment. ISS must be just one component of the school's safety and discipline strategies, with clearly defined rules and procedures, monitoring, and student help built in. If ISS consists of merely placing problem students in a room all day and forbidding them to speak, it will be no more successful than sending students home. Of course, in-school suspension requires additional staff time, school space, and planning, and may not be appropriate for all students.

• *Expulsion.* The last resort for schools, expulsion should be reserved for the most serious offenses and threatening situations. Rules regarding expulsion should be explained to all at the school and applied fairly. As with suspension, however, some districts exercise this option far more than others, and some expel disproportionately high numbers of minority students (Florida DOE, 1992; Silva, 1992). Schools and districts can request comparison data on expulsion rates in their states (from district or state department of education offices) to see if their expulsion practices and rates are within state norms.

> Expulsion should be reserved for the most serious offenses and threatening situations.

Many districts have no special programs for expelled students, who are simply turned out into the street to become the responsibility of law enforcement. Unfortunately, there are few community-sponsored programs for disruptive and/or disturbed youth. Again, punishment without attempting to address the source of the problem succeeds only in moving the problem elsewhere. Some districts have instituted alternative schools for their most disruptive and dangerous students. This approach provides specialized assistance for expelled and other problem students and relieves a burden from "regular" schools.

Districts may choose to have a clinical psychologist conduct evaluations of students who are considered a present danger to others. A written diagnosis from this authority can buttress a school's effort to have such students separated from others and given help and education on an individual basis.

Alternatives to Suspension—Dealing with Less Serious Incidents

Most schools seek alternatives to suspension when violent incidents are not severe enough to warrant removing the student. Described below, the most successful of these approaches often focus on building self-esteem and having students assume responsibility for the school and community. Section II discusses additional alternatives to suspension, including counseling and other long-term approaches to preventing violence.

• *Service Assignments.* Many schools give students an option of performing supervised assignments on school grounds in lieu of out-of-school suspension. Both the student and his or her parents must agree to this arrangement; also, students must not be allowed to work with heavy machinery. Service assignments can bring out significant benefits to all involved when handled properly. On an immediate level, they can save some students from the automatic failure which would result from missing several days of classes due to suspension. The students would work only during their elective class periods or before and after school. (Making students work through all their classes sends the wrong message: it tells students that the school is more interested in getting free labor than educating.) In addition, students can be given assignments which give them some responsibility and opportunities for success. Assignments of this type may involve:

Students prone to self-destructive behavior have been shown to make great strides as a result of engaging in activities that benefit others.

- serving as hall monitors,
- working in the office,
- removing graffiti,
- helping with landscaping, painting, restoration work,
- tutoring younger students

(Task Force on School Discipline, 1990)

Students must be supervised at all times. Assignments of this type are designed to be challenging and rewarding instead of punitive or humiliating. Students working on these projects are told that they are contributing to their school or community and are praised for their effort. It is important that students not be saddled with drudgery work which they will dislike or which will embarrass them in front of their peers. Low self-esteem is a major contributing problem with many violent students; the right kinds of work assignments can help to give students a chance to be proud of themselves. Staff volunteers can work with the students, cultivate positive relationships with them, and provide informal counseling.

Students prone to self-destructive behavior have been shown to make great strides as a result of engaging in activities

that benefit others. Well-planned service projects give at-risk
students the opportunity to

- develop higher self-esteem;
- develop values;
- practice job skills;
- bond with family, school, and community;
- interact with people from a wide range of social, racial, and economic backgrounds;
- get involved in activities that encourage expression and constructive risk (art, theater, music, etc.); and
- interact with the larger world and realize that they can help others.

(Follman et al., 1992)

Because service projects usually require a lot of organization and planning, and many of the benefits of the service
projects (to the students) are tied closely to their participation
in this planning, most service projects are more properly em-
ployed as a long-term preventive strategy to prevent and reduce
student violence; see Section II for a more extended discussion.

• *Alternative Educational Programs.* Some students, especially those with a history of disruptive and/or violent behavior,
may benefit from removal from the regular school and place-
ment in an alternative educational program. Alternative schools
and schools-within-schools emphasize independent study, good
conduct, and developing self-discipline and responsibility
(Table 5). Several models exist, including community-centered
schools that focus on group cohesiveness, family involvement,
and academic and social skills; adjustment schools for habitu-
ally disruptive or truant students; and apprenticeship programs
that prepare students for employment (NSSC, 1990a; Scrimger
& Elder, 1981).

• *Corporal Punishment.* Although corporal punishment has
long been used as a discipline strategy in this country, it is not
recommended as an alternative to suspension. A large body of
research indicates that the disadvantages of hitting children out-
weigh any possible benefits. Corporal punishment contributes
to the perception that striking another person is acceptable as a
problem-solving strategy (CDC, 1992) and it has little, if any,
lasting effect on promoting self-discipline (U. S. Department of

Justice, 1986). Striking a child as punishment in no way addresses the underlying causes of the child's act and occasionally results in physical injuries for which the school can be held liable.

Although the U. S. Supreme Court ruled in 1977 that corporal punishment is allowable in schools, 23 states and many districts in other states have banned its use (CDC, 1992; U. S. Department of Justice, 1986). Thousands of schools around the nation have reduced or are phasing out corporal punishment. Schools trying to reduce violence may have great difficulty justifying the use of corporal punishment as a deterrent to further violence. In addition, parents are more and more likely to challenge schools which use corporal punishment.

Table 5

Characteristics of Effective Alternative Educational Programs for Disruptive Youth

- Selection of program by student from several options provided by the school district, human services department, probation agency, or the courts
- Clear and consistent goals for students and parents
- Curricula addressing cultural and learning style differences
- High standards and expectations of student performance both academically and behaviorally
- Direct supervision of all activities on a closed campus
- Full-day attendance with rigorous workload and minimal time off
- Daily attendance and informal progress reports
- Continual monitoring and evaluation and formalized passage from one step or program to another
- A democratic climate
- A motivated and culturally diverse staff
- Counseling for parents and students
- Administrative and community support for the program

(Garrison, 1987, p. 22)

REFERENCES

Blauvelt, P. D. (1981). *Effective strategies for school security.* Reston, VA: National Association of Secondary School Principals.

Blauvelt, P. D. (1992, April). No title. Presentation for the Drug Free Schools Recognition Program, Washington, DC.

Blount, E. C. (1986). *Model guidelines for effective police-public school relationships.* Springfield, IL: Charles C. Thomas.

California State Department of Education. (1989). *Safe schools: A planning guide for action.* Sacramento, CA: Author.

Centers for Disease Control. (1992). *The prevention of youth violence: A framework for community action.* Atlanta: Division of Injury Control.

Ciminillo, L. M. (1980). Principal roles and school crime management. *NASSP Bulletin, 64*(433), 81–90.

Comerford, D. L., & Jacobson, M. G. (1987, April). *Suspension—Capital punishment for misdemeanors: The use of suspension at four suburban junior high schools and viable alternatives that could work.* Paper presented at the annual meeting of the American Educational Research Association, Washington, DC.

Dade County Public Schools. (1988). *Procedures for promoting and maintaining a safe learning enviroment.* Miami, FL: Office of Alternative Education.

Florida Department of Education. (1992). *1991 Florida youth risk behavior survey report.* Tallahassee, FL: Prevention Center.

Follman, J., Kelley, M., Hammond, C., & Tebo, M. (1992). *Learning by serving: A guide to service-learning and other youth community service programs.* Tallahassee: Florida Department of Education, Prevention Center.

Fulton County School System. (1991). *Crisis communication plan.* Atlanta: Information and Community Relations.

Garrison, R. (1987). Alternative schools get new recognition, results. *School Safety,* Fall, 22.

Gaustad, J. (1991). Schools respond to gangs and violence [Special issue]. *Oregon School Study Council (OSSC) Bulletin, 34*(9).

Greenbaum, S., Gonzalez, B., & Ackley, N. (1989). *Educated public relations: School safety 101.* Malibu, CA: National School Safety Center.

Greenbaum, S., Turner, B., & Stephens, R.D. (1989). *Set straight on bullies.* Malibu, CA: National School Safety Center.

Guidelines for policies addressing sexual misconduct toward students in public schools. (1992). Tallahassee: Florida Department of Education.

Hodgkinson, H. (1993). *Southern crossroads: A demographic look at the Southeast.* (Available from SERVE, 345 S. Magnolia Drive, Suite D-23, Tallahassee, FL 32301-2950 (800) 352-6001.)

National School Safety Center. (1990a). *School crisis prevention and response.* Malibu, CA: Author.

National School Safety Center. (1990c). *Weapons in schools.* Malibu, CA: Author.

Prophet, M. (1990). Safe schools in Portland. *The American School Board Journal, 177*(10), 28–30.

Rapp, J. A., Carrington, F., & Nicholson, G. (1992). *School crime and violence: Victims' rights.* Malibu, CA: National School Safety Center.

Silva, T. (1992, August 16). Does suspending students help or hurt? *Gainesville Sun,* 1A, 4A.

Speck, M. (1992, May). *Tokay high school proactive school safety plan.* Paper presented at the National School Safety Conference, Seattle, WA.

Task Force on School Discipline. (1990). *Report of the Task Force on School Discipline.* Tallahassee: Florida Department of Education.

U. S. Department of Justice. (1986). *Reducing school crime and student misbehavior: A problem-solving strategy.* Washington, DC: Author, National Institute of Justice.

Wehlage, G., & Rutter, R. (1986). Dropping out: How much do schools contribute to the problem? *Teacher's College Record, 87*(3).

Wheelock, A. (1986, November). *The way out: Student exclusion practices in Boston middle schools.* Boston: Massachusetts Advocacy Center.

Action Plans for Specific School Emergencies

by Stephanie Kadel and Joseph Follman

I n addition to having a general plan for dealing with violent emergencies, it can be useful for schools to develop strategies for coping with specific crises which could arise on the school campus. School safety committees can develop defined responses for such contingencies and hand them out to all staff and faculty members. Staff and faculty should review and update such plans annually.

> **It can be useful for schools to develop strategies for coping with specific crises.**

CIVIL DISTURBANCE

1. Encourage teachers and staff to be sensitive to the emotional climate of the campus and attempt to defuse any tensions prior to eruption of problems.
2. Notify on-site law enforcement of the disturbance and meet at a pre-designated site to evaluate the situation.
3. Have on-site law enforcement evaluate and call law enforcement agency for any necessary resources such as back-up help, emergency medical help, etc.
4. Activate needed emergency plans, which may include:
   a. Instructing office staff to man communications and initiate lockdown orders.
   b. Notifying transportation to bring appropriate numbers of buses for evacuation or transportation.
   c. Assigning staff to a temporary detention facility, such as a gymnasium, to secure students and log information.

From *Hot Topics: Usable Research, Reducing School Violence,* the SouthEastern Regional Vision for Education, 1993, p. 86–87. Reprinted with permission.

    d. Directing teachers to initiate lockdown and immo bilize the campus.

    e. Briefing a representative to meet the media.

    f. Assigning staff to a pre-designated medical treat ment/triage facility.

5. Notifying guidance counselor(s).

6. Conveying information at debriefing.

STAFF ASSAULT/BATTERY

1. Notify principal or designee.
2. Notify law enforcement.
3. Secure medical assistance as needed.
4. Identify assailant(s) and victim(s). Isolate assailants in predetermined location.
5. Report incident/injuries to district office.
6. Notify guidance office to address students' counseling needs.
7. Have a replacement ready for teacher victim's classes.
8. Meet with faculty and staff if necessary to defuse rumors.

STUDENT WITH A WEAPON

1. Do not confront the student.
2. Notify law enforcement and district office at once.
3. Identify the student, the student's location, and location of the weapon.
4. Have the on-site law enforcement officer or designee determine the level of threat:

If the level of threat is HIGH:

    call for back-up

    attempt to get the weapon from the student through negotiation

    take appropriate law enforcement action

If the level of threat is LOW:

    call the student to the office

    have law enforcement officer take appropriate action

UNAUTHORIZED PERSON ON CAMPUS

1. Post permanent signs affixed at all parking area entrances directing visitors to the office.
2. Post signs at campus building entrances instructing visitors to obtain a visitor ID badge at the front office.
3. Ask staff and faculty to question/challenge unauthorized persons (and students without passes) on campus.
4. Determine whether the person is a legitimate visitor or a threat to campus safety.
5. Escort legitimate visitors to the office to sign in and obtain a badge.
6. If a person on campus is suspected of posing a threat, have faculty or staff attempt to VOLUNTARILY escort the person to the front office. Notify or have a designee notify immediately the law enforcement officer on campus.
7. If a hostile confrontation is imminent, direct teachers to call the front office and notify law enforcement either on campus or by calling 911.
8. Instruct teachers not to engage in a violent confrontation; they should take every other step to ensure their safety and that of their students.
10. Instruct students, faculty, and staff to report any armed persons immediately.

(*School Campus Critical Incident/Violence Action Plan*, 1992)

What to Do When the Crisis Is Over

by Carter Burns

When tragedy strikes your school, a crisis-preparedness plan can help you put the pieces back together.

Picking up the pieces after violence strikes is one of the most troubling challenges schools face. Last year, a high school student in Olathe, Kan., threatened his girlfriend at school and was suspended for his actions. Less then 30 hours later, the young man stabbed the girl to death at her home, in front of her stepfather. The crime itself and the well-publicized court case that followed made a tremendous impact on everyone at Olathe North High School. As principal of the school at the time, it was up to me to help teachers respond to students' distress—and help the school community put the pieces back together.

> **Violent incidents no longer can be considered the exception.**

The case—and others like it—raises important issues for school boards: How do you ensure your schools can handle the aftermath of such a crisis? How do you know staff members are prepared to respond to this kind of trauma?

The incident at Olathe North High School is but one example of violence occurring all too regularly in schools and among students and teachers across the U.S. According to a recent *USA Weekend* survey of 23,300 students from age 10 to 16, 22 percent of the students said they don't feel safe at school. Forty percent said something violent happened in their schools during the past year.

From *The Amercan School Board Journal*, vol. 177, no. 3, p. 31–32, March 1990. Reprinted with permission.

The stark reality is this: For your schools and every school across the U.S., violent incidents no longer can be considered the exception. The only way to prepare for a violence-induced crisis in your school system—abrupt and unexpected as such incidents always are—is to develop a crisis-preparedness policy. That policy should set the stage for developing procedures that teachers and administrators should follow in the event of violence or death.

On the basis of my experience in Olathe, here are some guidelines your board might find useful in developing a crisis preparedness plan:

> **Teachers should allow—even encourage—students to discuss their reactions, focusing on feelings, not opinions.**

• **Get the facts.** A designated administrator (usually from the central office) should obtain substantiated facts about the incident and be responsible for making all public announcements. That person also should make sure board and staff members are fully informed. That might mean holding a staff meeting first thing in the school day, before classes begin, to give everyone the information they need.

• **Inform students.** The principal should encourage teachers to acknowledge the incident openly and honestly if students bring it up. It's important to tell youngsters the facts, in age-appropriate terms and (this is critical) without offering unnecessary details.

• **Discuss reactions.** Teachers should allow—even encourage—students to discuss their reactions, focusing on feelings, not opinions. Students also should have an opportunity to express their thoughts in writing. Your staff should be prepared for a wide range of emotional reaction: Not all students will respond to bad news with sorrow or remorse. Some will feel ambivalent and might hide their sense of shock or loss beneath a facade of jocularity or insensitivity. It's best to provide in-service training to help teachers develop the necessary skills for handling such situations.

• **Provide trained counselors.** Teachers should explain to youngsters that they might feel flooded with waves of emotion and that a counselor, social worker, or psychologist is available to help them. Students who are having extra difficulty especially need to see one of these experts. Indeed, teachers might want and need counseling themselves from support-staff professionals.

• **Find ways to comfort children.** If teachers feel at ease touching and hugging students, physical contact might well comfort distressed youngsters. Also, it's important that staff members recognize and respect students' varying religious beliefs. In crisis, many children—like adults—fall back on these beliefs for support.

• **Provide follow-up.** Reactions to crises often last a long time or recur long afterwards (for example, on anniversaries of the traumatic incident). Staff members should be prepared to provide follow-up counseling and discussion as students need help.

Whatever procedures your administrators establish for dealing with death, violence, or threats of violence, make sure parents are informed. Special parent meetings or newsletters can educate parents on the procedures and services available. In turn, you'll find that parents, students, and other community members will notify the schools when a student or staff member has faced a crisis away from school.

It's impossible for your schools to avoid outside crime or violence. But it's essential to be ready when crisis occurs. Most important, you should be prepared to communicate the message that your schools' first concern is the health, safety, and emotional well-being of students.

Plan procedures for responding to violence

Violent incidents can happen to students or staff members at school or away. In either case, teachers and administrators need to know how to respond.

Suppose a person is seen walking on campus with a weapon. Procedures must spell out how teachers will keep students in their classrooms under direct supervision until the threat is gone. It's wise to have a way to inform teachers of the possible danger without unnecessarily frightening students.

For example, the principal can make some sort of prearranged announcement over the intercom: "Due to an emergency, the bells will be shut off, and teachers will be notified when to dismiss their classes." Teachers will know to lock the classroom door and cover windows or interior walls so no one can look into the room.

Staff members also need directions on how to deal with a student or someone else carrying a weapon in school. In most cases, if no one is in imminent danger, staff members should not confront the person. Rather, a staff member should notify the building administrator who should call the police. The police should confront and arrest the individual.

Teachers also need to know how to respond to fighting, mugging, or other violent incidents in the school building. Some of the considerations that might determine whether to intervene: whether weapons are in use, the size of the combatants, the intensity of the situation, whether the teacher recognizes the combatants, the safety of other students nearby, and whether assistance is available. In many cases, it's wise for a teacher simply to supervise and observe rather than physically intervene and try to stop the altercation.

Procedures also should outline how to respond to death at school, at home, or in the community. (For guidelines on dealing with suicide, refer to *Responding to Student Suicide: The First 48 Hours*, a Current Issues Memo from Phi Delta Kappa International, September 1988.) Whether the death is a suicide or the result of a violent incident, it's important to provide accurate information to parents, students, and community and to make professional counseling available to anyone who needs it.—C.B.

Dealing with Violence and Threats of Violence in the School

by David Frisby and Joseph Beckham

In today's increasingly violent society, principals might want to be informed about how much force is appropriate to use in confrontations with students. A police official and former teacher provide an overview of general guidelines.

Violence in schools is a fact of life in some communities. Newspapers report instances of weapons in the possession of middle schoolers, assaults in high school classes, and attacks on teachers. While such events are often exaggerated in popular accounts, every administrator familiar with an act of violence in the school carries a sense of anticipatory dread that it could happen in his or her school.

> In some settings, the potential for violence justifies the regular presence of a law enforcement officer at the school.

In some settings, the potential for violence justifies the regular presence of a law enforcement officer at the school. Competent, well-trained school resource officers will be knowledgeable about the appropriate responses for dealing with resistance and violent conduct. These officers understand that response in a confrontational setting must be guided by a "continuum of force" standard of care.[1] Most state police academies teach a state-sanc-

From *NASSP Bulletin*, vol. 77, no. 552, p. 10–15, April 1993. Reprinted with permission.

tioned version of this continuum, and a resource officer should be able to provide details on local standards.[2]

Application of the response options regarded by local authorities as appropriate to a given set of circumstances reduces the risk of liability for the use of force in controlling students, and increases the likelihood that an explosive situation can be brought under control. Principals should be familiar with this standard of care, and should apply the standard when supervising or evaluating the performance of school resource officers.

RESISTANCE TO AUTHORITY

To understand the continuum of force, it is necessary to identify six categories or levels that violence or threats of violence can take (Figure 1). At a fundamental level, a student's very presence in a prohibited area may be a form of resistance. At the second level, a student may engage in verbal resistance. The third level of resistance—when a student resists the action or direction given—is usually called passive physical resistance. A fourth level of resistance is active resistance, and includes pulling away or fleeing. The fifth level of resistance is aggressive physical resistance, as when the student turns his active resistance against the person who is attempting to assert control. Finally, the sixth level of resistance is that of aggravated physical resistance, defined as resistance likely or intended to cause injury.

Figure 1
Resistance Levels

	Category	Definition	Example
6	Aggravated Physical	Resistance intended to or likely to cause injury	An attack with a weapon
5	Aggressive Physical	Resistance directed against a lawful authority	A push or a strike that does not cause injury
4	Active Physical	Resistance that is active and energetic in nature	Pulling away or running away
3	Passive Physical	Resistance that is passive and static in nature	Refusal to follow a lawful order
2	Verbal	Resistance that is spoken	Verbal defiance or spoken refusal to obey
1	Presence	Resistance in the form of presence or occurrence in an unauthorized place	A trespass by a student from a different school or by a suspended student

---

Figure 2
Police Response

	Category	Definition/Example
1	Police Presence	Arrival, interview stance
2	Verbal Control	Dialog, verbal direction, touch (consoling)
3	Touch Control	Restraint devices, pain compliance, take downs, countermoves, transporters
4	Intermediate Weapons	Specialty weapons: mace, baton
5	Incapacitating Control	Stunning blows, neck restraints
6	Deadly Force	Firearms, vehicles

RESPONSE LEVELS

Just as there are six levels of resistance, law enforcement authorities identify six levels of response (Figure 2). From the options on the continuum, an officer is expected to use only that level of response necessary to control the situation. Thus, at an initial level, the officer must establish presence. This can be done by announcing his authority or presenting himself in uniform. Presence is often enough force to obtain compliance.

The second level of force is verbal direction. Requesting or commanding, verbally or with body language, in a forceful, direct, and clear manner, may be sufficient to end a threat of misconduct.

A third level of force is touch control. Touch control may involve a range of options for the law enforcement official, and is one of the most complex levels of force. Subcategories within the level of response might include holds and grips designed to control or move the individual, or take downs used to place the individual on the ground. This category might also include the use of restraints such as handcuffs, or reactive techniques such as blocks and strikes designed to control but not incapacitate.

The fourth level of force is alternate weapons, which might include police batons, police mace, and stun guns. The appropriate use of these weapons at this level requires specialized training and knowledge to effectively obtain compliance. Sloppy, inappropriate use of these weapons will usually justify a higher force classification when reviewed.

Incapacitating force is the fifth level of response. This level emphasizes temporary incapacitation through the use of techniques that might include strikes and blows, or the controversial police technique of the choke hold.

Level six is the use of deadly force. Such force would be likely to cause serious bodily harm or death, and would include baton strikes to the head or discharge of a firearm.

> An officer is expected to use only that level of response necessary to control the situation.

RESPONSE VS. RESISTANCE

The relationship between each level of resistance and the level of response is presented in a "continuum of force" matrix in Figure 3. Law enforcement officials in local communities may vary their continuum of force policies, although certain general guidelines will likely apply. The officer may respond to resistance at any indicated level, but once compliance is achieved, he or she must de-escalate as much as possible, consistent with maintaining control. Further, there must be an articulable reason as to why the lesser level of force would not be effective if the officer bypasses the recommended levels in the continuum matrix.

There are other legal theories authorizing the use of force. "Force to prevent a crime" is an example. However, the general trend in civil accountability is to acknowledge the "continuum of force."

APPLICATION TO THE ADMINISTRATOR

A decision to use a level of force that exceeds a level necessary to control a situation in a school setting may be considered excessive, and may carry with it the potential for criminal or civil liability.[3] School and law enforcement officials are typically held to a standard of reasonable force in situations in which force is used to effect compliance. The law allows only that force which is reasonably necessary to effectively bring an incident under control.[4] Knowledge and application of response levels to the level of resistance offered affords a guide to the standard of reasonableness that might be adopted by a court when reviewing the force used to control a situation involving students.

A decision to use a level of force to control a school situation that is significantly below the highest level suggested by the continuum of force standard will always be praised when it is successful. In those cases where the level of force used is below that suggested and the force fails to control the violence, critics and injured parties may wish to place blame and seek redress from "deep pocket" agencies through their chief administrators.

> **A decision to use a level of force below the highest level … will always be praised when it is successful.**

Without knowledge of these techniques and the existing standard of care, school officials may employ tactics that are inappropriate, ineffective, or excessive, aggravating or escalating a confrontational situation. Legal liability could result, in addition to the bad publicity that accompanies campus problems.

Although weapons training for school administrators seems far fetched, the administrator must have access to a variety of techniques that allow him or her to respond to acts of violence in a school setting. Skills in verbal persuasion are obviously critical. Unarmed self-defense tactics, the use of come-along holds and restraint, and physical compliance measures may ultimately become part of a school administrator's repertoire.

In any case, school administrators charged with the duty to establish and implement policies for the effective supervision of students and employees must have knowledge of the continuum of force. Administrators are routinely held accountable for the safety of students and the supervision of employees. Thus, a school policy on "use of force" that parallels state standards will provide insulation from liability as well as much needed guidance to employees in situations involving violence or threats of violence.

Figure 3
Use of Force/Levels of Resistance Matrix

	6 Aggravated Physical	5 Aggressive Physical	4 Active Physical	3 Passive Physical	2 Verbal	1 Presence
Deadly Force — Deadly Force 6	X					
Incap. Control 5 — Incapacitation	X	X				
Inter. Weapon Control 4 — Intermediate Weapons	X	X	X			
Physical Control 3 — Countermoves	X	X	X			
Pain Compliance	X	X	X	X		
Take Downs	X	X	X	X		
Transporters	X	X	X	X		
Restraint Devices	X	X	X	X	X	
Verbal Control 2 — Dialog	X	X	X	X	X	
Verbal Direction	X	X	X	X	X	X
Touch (consoling)	X	X	X	X	X	X
Police Presence 1 — Interview Stance	X	X	X	X	X	X
Arrival	X	X	X	X	X	X

Note: Checked areas represent suggested, acceptable, beginning response levels. Any response in an unchecked area requires explanation.

NOTES

1. Missy K. O'Linn, Esq., "The Gaps in Use-of-Force Policies and Training," *The Police Chief*, February 1992.

2. Florida Department of Law Enforcement Division of Criminal Justice Standards and Training, *Florida Defensive Tactics Training*, 1990.

3. See, e.g., Shorba v. Board of Educ., 583 P.2d 213 (Haw. 1978); Williams v. Cotton, 346 So.2d 1039 (Fla. Dist. Ct. App. 1977); and Dodd v. State, 126 S.W. 834 (Ark. 1910).

4. See e.g., Gaspershon v. Harnett County Bd. of Educ., 330 S.E.2d 489 (N.C. Ct. App. 1985); Owens v. Commonwealth, 473 S.W.2d 827 (Ky. 1963); and Hogan v. Newton, 56 N.Y.S.2d 779 (N.Y. 1945).

Safe Streets in Tacoma

by Mary Nebgen

When gang violence hit Tacoma, Wash., school officials, police, and community leaders banded together to keep city streets safe.

You could say life in the Tacoma, Wash. schools was pretty peaceful until September 1988. Sure, discipline problems occurred in the 32,000-student district, but those problems rarely involved students bringing drugs or weapons onto school grounds.

Sadly, however, that changed. After that September, discipline problems increased in number and seriousness. We documented 68 cases of weapons on campus during the 1988-89 school year—twice as many as the year before. Substance abused increased dramatically. And some students began wearing blue or red caps, bandannas, and jackets—attire known to signify membership in local gangs.

Schools weren't the only part of the community affected. Police in Tacoma and surrounding Pierce County grew alarmed at the situation on the streets. Gang membership had increased three-fold, and there were 1,000 known crack houses in the county. Dealers sold heroin, cocaine, and crack openly. Between 1987 and 1988, homicides doubled, violent crime rose 78 percent, and juvenile prosecutions for weapon-related offenses jumped from eight to 120. And in 1988, 75 drive-by shootings resulted in 40 injuries and four deaths.

At first, community members expressed disbelief, then alarm. The same question was on everyone's mind: How could the escalating crime and violence be stopped?

From *The American School Board Journal,* vol. 177, no. 10, p. 26–27, October 1990. Reprinted with permission.

JOINING FORCES

An answer began to materialize when, by chance, a county council member, a school official, and the director of the county's juvenile detention center met on an out-of-town trip in the fall of 1988. After discussing the problem, they decided to call a meeting of law enforcement leaders, schools officials, legislators, and heads of various community groups.

All participants agreed that any response to the gang, drug, and violence problem had to be well-organized and comprehensive. The result was a consortium made up of the Tacoma schools; city, county, and state governments; and the United Way and private contributors. All the consortium members pledged financial support. To head the effort, the consortium hired Lyle Quasim, a respected community leader, to serve as director. The Safe Streets Campaign was under way.

> All participants agreed that any response to the gang, drug, and violence problem had to be well-organized and comprehensive.

As the first order of business, Quasim called a public meeting to hear citizens' suggestions about how to attack the problem. More than 2,000 people attended, gathering in groups to discuss common fears and complaints: neighborhood crack houses, drug peddlers who approached children, gang influences in schools, and a perception that the courts were too easy on drug criminals. Suggested solutions ranged from the simplistic ("make schools teach the law") to the modestly practical ("provide more after-school activities for kids").

With hundreds of suggestions in hand, Safe Streets leaders went on retreat to begin to shape a comprehensive action plan. They came back with a strategy that involves eight segments of the community. The efforts of all eight are coordinated and assisted by the Safe Streets Campaign, but, as the following list shows, each segment has its own contribution to make:

1. **Community organizations.** Service clubs, block-watch organizations, and parent-teacher groups identify vacant and rental properties in imperiled neighborhoods and work with owners and landlords to prevent the properties from becoming crack houses. To help the police, citizens in expanded block-watch programs report illegal drug activity. They organize cam-

paigns to beautify neighborhoods, removing graffiti and sweeping the streets. They march and picket to protest crack houses and sponsor drug-free days and block parties that help neighbors get to know each other.

2. **Schools.** The school system pays six off-duty police officers to patrol high school grounds for three hours every day from lunch period through dismissal.
Schools ban student beepers, pagers, and gang-related apparel and work to remove gang graffiti from school walls. The school board has revised discipline policies on drugs and weapons and has adopted a "no tolerance" stance that calls for immediate expulsion of violators. School officials have lobbied for legislation that would increase penalties for any drug-related violation occurring within 1,000 feet of a school.

> To help the police, citizens in expanded block-watch programs report illegal drug activity.

In addition, school officials have bolstered health and substance-abuse programs at all levels. Various clubs—including the Rotary, Elks, Optimists, Kiwanis, and Lions—have donated funds or time to such programs in elementary and middle schools. The police department sponsors the DARE program in six elementary and middle schools. (DARE—Drug Abuse Resistance Education—brings police officers to schools to teach students about substance abuse-prevention.)

School officials also have expanded intervention and support programs. The Rotary Club finds support groups for at-risk elementary and middle school students. Using grant money, educators have trained selected middle school staff members in how to recognize drug use among students and how to intervene. Two high schools contract for services from an adolescent treatment facility. Four high schools have their own "after-care" classes—support groups for students who have been through formal treatment. A district-produced, parent-education video called "It Can Happen In Any Family" is available to PTAs. Substance abuse prevention agencies offer a 10-hour workshop for parents on how to reinforce skills their children learn in class.

3. **Businesses.** Tacoma businesses pay uniformed security guards to patrol downtown streets to reduce illegal activity. In

addition, they have provided mentors and summer jobs to young people from high-risk neighborhoods, donated employee time to clean up their business neighborhoods, sponsored Safe Streets promotional materials, and provided free equipment and supplies for campaign projects. The Chamber of Commerce has initiated new school-business partnerships, concentrating on schools in high-crime areas. In collaboration with the school system, the businesses pay for someone to oversee the partnership efforts.

> City and county council members ride along with police officers to learn firsthand the realities of the streets.

4. **Government agencies.** The courts, city and county governments, and city and county police departments are using several strategies to attack the problem. They provide seminars to city and county officials to increase awareness of drug activity and gang violence. City and county council members ride along with police officers to learn firsthand the realities of the streets. A Crime Watch program trains citizens to recognize crime and report suspected illegal drug activity. And a 24-hour police hot line lets citizens report suspected crack houses.

5. **Labor groups.** Local unions and other labor organizations give out information on substance abuse to employees. Working with the Safe Streets Campaign, the labor groups have held programs on preventing substance abuse. Members volunteer for Safe Streets projects, such as restoring houses. They support mentor programs for at-risk youth through the local vocational-technical schools.

6. **Youth.** In March 1989, 2,500 area high school students gathered at the University of Puget Sound for a Safe Streets Youth Forum. Presenters from the National Crime Council and the National Drug Enforcement Agency, as well as the police chief and other community experts, discussed drugs, gangs, and crime with small groups of students. The youngsters then came up with possible solutions, such as expansion of drug education programs, public funding of worthwhile youth programs, and stiffer penalties for drug possession and selling. High school students now organize and participate in cleanup efforts for local communities. They run peer-counseling programs for youth

at risk of gang and drug involvement, recognize youth involved in anti-drug and anti-gang activity, and encourage the news media to highlight young people's positive contributions. They also work in the Safe Streets management office and help recruit volunteers.

7. **Religious organizations.** Several religious groups conduct a Religious Summit and organize peaceful marches through areas known for heavy drug traffic. During one of these marches, religious leaders laid crosses at spots where person had died from drug-related violence—a symbolic and somber recognition of the extent of the problem. Local religious groups also sponsor programs for at-risk youth, operate an expanded ministry at juvenile detention facilities, and raise funds to purchase abandoned property in troubled neighborhoods. With the help of business and labor organizations, these properties are rehabilitated and given to low-income families.

> More than 2,000 citizens are involved in the Safe Streets Campaign.

8. **Prevention and treatment agencies.** Substance-abuse agencies help schools identify, assess, and refer students who might need treatment. Tacoma schools now have core teams trained to recognize symptoms of drug abuse and get help for students. They also hold public forums on drug abuse.

EARLY SUCCESSES

Tacoma saw an alarming rise in what are increasingly common problems of our time—drug abuse, gangs, and violence. The initial reaction of the community was fright and anger. But the Safe Streets Campaign has calmed those emotions and united the community in a practical effort to eliminate the problem. The effort is based on the belief that the community can achieve success if its various elements work together with determination and good sense.

More than 2,000 citizens are involved in the Safe Streets Campaign. But will it all work? It's too soon to give a definitive answer: The campaign is just two years old, but it already has been successful in closing several crack houses, eliminating gang graffiti from certain sections of town, rehabilitating some properties, and persuading some landlords to renovate others. Everyone has reason to hope the campaign will achieve its long-term goal—to eradicate the city's drug and gang activity through coordinated community efforts.

Tell Teen Gangs: School's Out

by Kenneth S. Trump

The time to protect your schools against youth gangs is before gangs get a firm foothold in your district.

Youth gangs, traditionally viewed as a concern only for urban school districts, can now be found in urban, suburban, and even rural schools. Many gang-related incidents start in the community but spill over into the schools. Regardless of the source of the problem, you must address these safety concerns first or your education programs will not be effective.

Gangs present a problem for you as a school leader because the development of a youth gang is a process, not a single event. Gang activity that is not dealt with promptly and effectively will become more entrenched as the gang attracts more students who seek the status that often goes along with gang membership. You will experience more problems by denying that gang issues exist than by acknowledging the impact of gang violence and making efforts to minimize its impact.

> **Gang activity that is not dealt with promptly and effectively will become more entrenched as the gang attracts more students.**

Our experience in the Cleveland Public Schools clearly demonstrates that both the gang problem and concerns about image can be successfully managed. We acknowledged the negative impact of gangs on the education environment by creating a gang intervention and prevention team in the district's Divi-

From *The American School Board Journal*, vol. 180, no. 7, p. 39–42, July 1993. Reprinted with permission.

sion of Safety and Security in late 1991. This five-officer Youth Gang Unit, which serves 127 schools with more than 73,000 students, contributed to a 39 percent reduction in school gang incidents (from 381 to 231) in its second year of operation.

This program has reduced school gang violence and helped give the district a more positive public image. By acknowledging the problem and taking action, we collected information that dispels many inaccurate myths and public perceptions. For example, drugs and weapons were perceived to be the biggest problem associated with gangs. Our findings show otherwise: The majority of school gang incidents were assaults (38 percent), fights and disruptive behavior (15 percent), threats and menacing words (14 percent), and trespassing (13 percent). Weapons accounted for 7 percent and drugs for only 3 percent of the total number of gang-related incidents in the Cleveland schools. By presenting these figures and explaining our strategies for addressing youth gangs to parents, the community, and the news media, we were able to improve the district's image in the area of school safety.

Signs to watch for

Often, telltale signs signal the presence of a youth gang in your school system. Be alert to these signs of possible gang involvement:

- **Colors:** Students who are involved in gangs often show a subtle or obvious choice of color in their clothes or wear specific brands or styles of sportswear, hats, shoes, bandannas, jewelry, and haircuts.
- **Graffiti:** Unusual signs, symbols, alphabets, and nicknames on notebooks, papers, clothing, and walls can be signals of gang activity.
- **Tattoos:** Students who have symbols or names tattooed on their arms, chest, or elsewhere on their bodies might be gang members.
- **Handsigns or handshakes:** Gang members often have unusual ways of signaling or greeting each other.
- **Language:** Students who use uncommon terms, words, names, or phrases might be signaling their membership in a gang.

> - **Initiations:** Suspicious or otherwise unexplained bruises, wounds, or injuries might be the result of gang initiation ceremonies.
> - **Behavior changes:** Sudden changes of mood or behavior, unexplained poor grades, and secretive friendships or meetings can signal gang involvement.—K.S.T.

Similar approaches can be used in school systems of varying sizes. Start by developing a set of policies and procedures for dealing with youth gangs in your school system and as part of the overall community. Your policies should include the use of carefully written and publicized student handbooks, staff training in gang prevention at both the building and district level, the development of community-wide strategies, and methods for dealing with the news media.

IS IT A GROUP OR A GANG?

It's not easy to identify a gang—especially during the early stages of a gang's formation, when its leadership and structure might be informal. During the teenage years, many students tend to run in packs and seem to find a certain comfort in looking and acting just like the rest of the crowd. A social group is one thing, however; a gang is something else entirely. A gang is defined by the negative behavior of its members: Kids who sit together in the lunchroom don't constitute a gang. But when groups start assaulting other students or creating an atmosphere of fear and intimidation, they become a gang. In short, groups of students reach gang status when their behavior, either individually or collectively, is disruptive, antisocial, or criminal.

The time to act is as soon as you see signs that gangs are forming in your district. Gang activity varies considerably from region to region, and each school system's response will need to vary accordingly. I cannot suggest blanket definitions or step-by-step plans, but one general rule holds true: Overreacting and resorting to extreme measures will do little to alleviate gang violence.

Instead, you'll have to develop a working definition and action plan locally, a plan you can implement relatively early to avoid the lag time that aids gang growth. Don't act alone. Involve police, social service, and community organizations in developing comprehensive strategies for dealing with gangs. Here are some of the factors to include in your plan.

THE DRESS CODE QUESTION

A dress code is an important part of your overall antigang effort, but it is far from the only component. (An effective policy targets gang behavior, not just the outward signs of gang membership.) Sometimes, demands from the community to halt school gang activities can pressure school boards into creating policies that focus almost exclusively on dress codes that ban certain colors, bandannas, or other insignia that identify gangs. Such policies are often outdated as soon as they are adopted.

> Strive for a policy that is general enough to adjust to the ever-changing, fluid nature of gang activity.

Instead of a dress code that is too narrow (or too vague) strive for a policy that is general enough to adjust to the ever-changing, fluid nature of gang activity. You can ban red, blue, and black bandannas, for example, but that rule won't help you if the gang members decide to wear green the day after you publish the dress code.

It's far safer to design a general school district policy that addresses appearance that is disruptive to the educational environment. Have your school attorney check the policy for legal soundness, and delegate to school principals the responsibility for defining specific dress regulations to meet their schools' needs.

In designing such policies, it is vital to take into account the constitutionality of restricting gang clothing in public schools. Writing in the Southern California *Law Review* in 1991, Paul D. Murphy offers a detailed review of First Amendment issues and suggests ways to design legally valid dress codes. Murphy cautions that dress codes, which should be capable of adapting to changing styles, should be used in conjunction with other gang prevention programs. He also recommends that policies provide for explaining a dress code to students before it goes into effect and issuing informal warnings to first-time and infrequent violators. (Murphy also advises schools to keep detailed documentation of problems and disruptions caused by gang confrontations and to ensure an unbiased appeals process at every level.)

RULES AND CONSEQUENCES

Your school system may minimize the need for policies that specifically address gangs if you have a comprehensive student handbook that identifies expectations for student behavior and outlines the consequences for all students who break the rules. Student handbooks should clearly outline student rights and responsibilities and should include a section on freedom of expression and dress codes. Be sure to explain suspension and expulsion procedures carefully and describe the appeals process. A well-written handbook can help ensure that all students are treated fairly, firmly and consistently.

> A well-written handbook can help ensure that all students are treated fairly, firmly and consistently.

Staff members should review and revise student handbooks each year, present them to students on the first day of each school year, and review them with students during assemblies and in each classroom. Each student should be asked to sign a receipt indicating that he or she received the handbook, and teachers should maintain lists of those signed receipts—an excellent way to counter students who say, "I never knew about that rule."

Administrators must understand that they need to reinforce their expectations for behavior, in addition to their academic expectations, at regular intervals throughout the school year. It's not enough to hold one assembly at the beginning of the school year and then remind students about the rules only when they are broken. Through your policies and procedures, encourage the staff to hold regular discussions of school safety issues and expectations for student behavior.

Steps your staff can take

Policies and procedures that decrease gang activity are best developed locally, to meet local needs. As you plan your school district's response to gang activity, keep the following suggestions in mind:

School administrators can:
- Identify schools as neutral ground and adopt a "no tolerance" policy for gang activity.
- Learn to distinguish between youthful misbehavior and crime.
- Train school personnel to identify and handle gang members.
- Create a mechanism for mediating student conflicts.
- Institute antigang and antidrug education programs.
- Establish cooperative relationships with police and social service personnel who serve your schools.

Teachers can:
- Treat all students fairly, firmly, and consistently.
- Incorporate gang issues into class lessons; address rights and responsibilities, decision making, and problem-solving skills.
- Report suspected gang involvement and activity to administrators.
- Establish good lines of communication with parents.
- Be aware of community resources that meet students' needs.—K.S.T.

TRAINING FOR GANG PREVENTION

In addition to publishing and reinforcing the rules in the student handbook, schools need an effective training program, which should include sessions for staff at both building and district levels. Educators often learn what little they know about gangs through the distorted lens of the entertainment industry. Too often, training programs focus almost exclusively on the sociology of gangs—or focus too much on gang graffiti or clothing. You'll need a balanced training program that reduces stereotypes and helps staff members approach gang issues rationally. Such training reduces overreaction by eliminating the fear of the unknown.

A training session for school staff should last at least two or three hours, during which you can discuss the formation and structure of gangs and examine gang identifiers, such as jewelry, haircuts, graffiti, and tattoos. Conclude the program with concrete recommendations for gang intervention and prevention strategies at the individual, classroom, and building levels. This format provides school administrators and teachers with a balanced overview of why gangs exist, how they are organized, and what the school can do once gangs are recognized.

One part of the training should be helping staff members understand the motivation for joining gangs. Young people often believe they get many benefits from being gang members. Gang membership can offer social and economic rewards such as power, status, money, security, friendship, and a substitute for family. Some students find excitement in dealing drugs and in being recognized as the "dope boy," an image some teens find glamorous.

> **One part of the training should be helping staff members understand the motivation for joining gangs.**

The training needs to emphasize that "Just say no" programs are too simple to be effective in preventing students from joining gangs. Instead, teachers must get students to weigh honestly the costs and benefits of belonging to a gang. For example, teachers might generate a discussion by saying: "Think of someone you knew five years ago who was gangbanging and dealing drugs. What has happened to that person?" Many students will recognize the long-term negative consequences of such behavior when exploring these issues through realistic class discussions.

Your policies should also encourage teachers and administrators to ask questions of groups of students who act suspiciously or who start wearing certain clothing or jewelry. If school personnel see nine or 10 students wearing the exact same heavy silver chains or displaying the same insignia on their notebooks, they should ask, "What does this mean?" Gangs often flourish because they feel anonymous and safe from the watchful eyes of adults.

Finally, urge teachers not to ignore opportunities for teaching about nonviolent ways to solve problems. If a teacher sees a fight in the hall, and the students' attention is focused on it, the teacher shouldn't simply shut the door and continue the math or science lesson as though the fight had never taken place. Instead, the teacher needs to address the reasons for the fight and ways to avoid such conflicts in the future.

At the district level, training should also emphasize policy and administrative implications. Communities beginning to acknowledge and act on gang issues should consider convening a training session for officials from city government, law enforcement, criminal justice, social service, and other youth service agencies. Such sessions can reduce stereotypes and fears—and give civic leaders an opportunity to develop a community-wide strategy and reach a common understanding of gang dynamics and prevention techniques.

How do you tell the press?

Youth gang activity will draw reporters' attention, and for that reason, your gang prevention plan should include procedures for dealing with the news media. The fact is, gangs and school violence make good stories, which means you and your administrators might be fielding many questions from the press about gang-related incidents in your schools.

Keep in mind that the news media will cover the issue with or without your consent or help, so it is best to cooperate. The worst possible thing you can say to a reporter is, "No comment." Instead, explain if you are investigating incidents but don't yet have all the details. Identify the steps you have taken or plan to take in general terms. Offer to get back to reporters with an answer if you need more time, but be sure you do get back to them.

Understand that reporters work under strict deadlines, and make a special attempt to be accessible, responsive, timely, and honest in answering their inquiries. At the same time, establish and communicate clear guidelines and expectations to your staff about dealing with the news media. Explain your media policy and procedures in advance to members of the press. Get to know reporters when there is no crisis by inviting them to cover positive events at your schools and by showing that you are dealing effectively with gangs and other problematic issues. By acknowledging the impact of social problems on your school system, and by identifying the positive steps you have taken to reduce and prevent these problems, you increase the likelihood that reporters will write balanced articles about your schools.—K.S.T.

HELP FROM SPECIALISTS

If gang problems have become entrenched in your school district, you might need to employ specialists—either a full-time staff member or a team of professionals—to deal exclusively with gang issues. In Cleveland, as I mentioned earlier, a special

Youth Gang Unit of the Division of Safety and Security of the Cleveland Public Schools has compiled an excellent record: Our schools have seen a 39 percent decrease in school gang-related incidents during the 1992-93 school year, compared to the year before.

> **Human and not mechanical intervention will ultimately change the negative behavior of gang members.**

This five-officer team, which I coordinate, receives training on a variety of issues, including gang organization, conflict mediation, and student rights and due process. The officers are responsible for enforcement and investigations, mediating gang conflicts, quelling rumors, and training staff, parents, and students on gang issues.

We also have an extremely cooperative relationship with the Cleveland Police Department's Youth/Gang unit. Together, the two units exchange intelligence on gang trends, conduct cooperative investigations, and target locations of frequent gang activity. Both units also work cooperatively with other criminal justice and social service agencies throughout the city to prevent youth gang crime and disruptions.

A similar approach might be just as effective in your school district. Some school districts—usually in response to high-profile incidents, community pressures, or costly legal action—implement security systems that use metal detectors, surveillance cameras, and other equipment. In my view, security equipment must serve as a support to, not a replacement for, professional security personnel. Human and not mechanical intervention will ultimately change the negative behavior of gang members and other young people who defy society's rules. Security equipment is best used in conjunction with a plan that addresses underlying issues; it should not be a quick fix to an incident that garnered negative press. School security professionals should be used to manage comprehensive programs that include safety policies and procedures, methods of investigating and reporting incidents, deployment of security personnel, physical security and many other components.

As a school leader, you must set aside all personal and political agendas that prevent you from dealing with youth gangs and other school safety concerns. School safety must be your

No. 1 priority, a priority that is reflected in your budget and programs.

Age of Reckoning

by Peter Schmidt

The facts are clear. Children are committing more serious crimes at younger ages. What isn't clear is what can and should be done about it. Experts across the country—from politicians to pundits—are proposing tough new laws to waive juvenile offenders to adult courts. But behind all the political rhetoric lie legal, ethical, and practical concerns about whose side such laws would really be on.

After a decade of promising to improve the education system, politicians have begun to embrace a new cure for what ails some children: the adult-criminal-justice system. Where they once spoke of helping children whom society has placed at risk, many now speak of incarcerating those who pose a risk to society. Threatening and imposing adult sentences, they claim, is the only way to make schools safe and drug-free. Pledging school reform has given way to lamenting the failure of reform schools.

In delivering their annual State of the State addresses over the past two months, the nation's governors have almost without exception focused on crime and, especially, the upsurge in violence committed by juveniles. Almost all have vowed to get tough, and many have proposed placing entire categories of juvenile offenders under the jurisdiction of adult courts.

"We must understand that our present system did not envision the level of violence and viciousness among young offenders today," said Gov. Zell Miller of Georgia. Calling for a

> Threatening and imposing adult sentences, they claim, is the only way to make schools safe and drug-free.

From *Education Week*, vol. 13, no. 24, p. 24–27, March 9, 1994. Reprinted with permission.

modernized state juvenile-justice system "to crack down on those young punks who commit violent crimes," Miller added that he would seek to have juveniles as young as age 13 tried as adults for such offenses.

Lawmakers in New York, Arizona, Washington, Florida, Minnesota, Illinois, and several other states have taken up similar measures.

On the national level, U.S. Attorney General Janet Reno has endorsed the approach used in her home state of Florida, which holds the threat of being treated as adults over young offenders to get them to cooperate with the juvenile system. Moreover, the U.S. Senate's anti-crime bill calls for children 13 and older to be automatically transferred to adult court for violent federal offenses.

In keeping with traditional approaches to juvenile delinquency, many of the new initiatives try to address societal problems linked to juvenile crime. Most of their proponents, however, clearly reject the belief that the prior victimization of serious juvenile criminals is reason to treat them more leniently.

"We sympathize with those neglected children who are tempted by drugs or gangs," declared Gov. Pete Wilson of California, who has called for violent offenders as young as 14 to be prosecuted as adults. "But when as teenagers or adults they victimize others, our sympathy must yield to responsibility. And our first responsibility must always be to protect the innocent and punish the guilty."

Gov. Fife Symington of Arizona contended that "there is every reason to question whether our courts should be moonlighting as social-service agencies." What's more, he added, "I was not hired to be Arizona's chief social theorist. I was not sent here to sit meditating on Freud or the latest 'root causes' of criminal behavior."

NO SIMPLE SOLUTIONS

Many experts on juvenile law criticize the wholesale transfer of certain juvenile offenders to adult courts as a simplistic, and potentially disastrous, solution to a complex problem. Such an approach, they say, does little to address the well-established antecedents of serious, violent, and chronic juvenile crime: neglect, weak family attachments, a lack of consistent discipline, poor school performance, delinquent peer groups, physical or sexual abuse, or an upbringing in high-crime neighborhoods.

"We have not valued millions of our children's lives, and so they do not value ours in a society in which they have no social or economic stake," Marian Wright Edelman, the president of the Children's Defense Fund, told a House subcommittee last month as she urged it to leave provisions calling for adult treatment of some categories of young offenders out of its crime bill.

Moreover, the leadership of the National Council of Juvenile and Family Court Judges argues that sending juvenile offenders to adult courts and prisons virtually destroys any hope for rehabilitation. Others cite research indicating that juveniles sentenced in adult courts tend to have higher recidivism rates and to commit another crime sooner after their release than those who go through the juvenile system.

> Sending juvenile offenders to adult courts and prisons virtually destroys any hope for rehabilitation.

Legal scholars also caution that changes in laws dealing with juvenile offenders may signal a major shift in society's overall conception of childhood and children's legal rights and responsibilities. This shift, they say, could have wide-ranging implications for other areas of law, as well as for school policies dictating discipline, governance, and the transfer of student records.

Barry C. Feld, a professor of law at the University of Minnesota, says our nation's changing view of childhood culpability and responsibility "has implications for every age-graded social institution in our society" and could influence our thinking on voting rights and juvenile due process, among other areas.

As the presiding judge of the juvenile court in Santa Clara County, Calif., Leonard P. Edwards has seen several school systems adopt mandatory-expulsion policies that bar children from schools for certain offenses.

Ronald D. Stephens, the executive director of the National School Safety Center in Westlake Village, Calif., says some states also have been changing their laws to give school administrators more access to the records of juveniles whose cases were processed by juvenile courts. He predicts that teacher access to such information will become a "major bargaining chip" in contract talks.

After all, teachers can often see the signs from an early age. "You hear elementary teachers say, 'This kid is going to kill somebody by the time he gets out of high school,'" says Lieut. William F. Balkwill, who runs the youth-services unit of the Sarasota County, Fla., sheriff's department. "Then, six or seven years later, it comes true."

> You hear elementary teachers say, 'This kid is going to kill some-body by the time he gets out of high school'...Then, six or seven years later, it comes true.

"We have begun to break down the dichotomy of 'child' and 'adult,' says Janet E. Ainsworth, a professor of law at the University of Puget Sound who has written on the subject. Our legal system, she notes, appears to be changing to account for a fact educators have long known: Children and adults are not separated by a single distinct line.

But when society sees the bill for incarcerating large new populations of juveniles, experts predict, it will likely begin putting more pressure on schools to pick up where families have failed. "It simply is not rational public policy to condition our willingness to spend money on children on their getting into trouble first," Edelman argued in her testimony.

ABANDONING TRADITION

The American juvenile-justice system sprouted from the establishment of separate juvenile courts and legal procedures more than a century ago.

According to Hunter Hurst III, the director of the National Center for Juvenile Justice, the Pittsburgh-based research branch of the National Council of Juvenile and Family Court Judges, the founders of the first juvenile courts envisioned a system that would guide loiterers, runaways, and young perpetrators of petty crimes toward a responsible and productive adulthood. To this day, juvenile judges say they seek to strike a balance between protecting the community, holding children and parents accountable for children's actions, and helping wayward youths develop the skills they need to get back on the right track.

However, law-enforcement and school officials also have long objected to the secrecy shrouding the proceedings of juvenile courts—a secrecy they say prevents consideration of a juvenile's previous record and hinders efforts to identify and track serious offenders.

By the 1970's, increases in the seriousness of much juvenile crime had prompted states to begin rethinking their juvenile-justice systems to establish provisions for sending certain cases to adult courts. By 1992, according to the National Center for Youth Law in San Francisco, every state had some mechanism for prosecuting youths under 18 as adults.

Despite such changes in state statutes, there remains a widespread perception that juvenile courts coddle young criminals and that those criminals have exploited this fact to unleash a growing onslaught of hard-core teenage crime.

> There remains a widespread perception that juvenile courts coddle young criminals.

"The statistics are telling," said Gov. Barbara Roberts of Oregon in announcing the formation of a task force to rethink that state's juvenile-justice system. "Nine out of 10 juveniles now in custody in Oregon are committed for felonies. One-third are committed for sexual offenses. Over the past five years, the number of homicide-related offenders in the juvenile system has grown 800 percent." Our society's failure to hold juveniles more responsible for their actions, she concluded, "is turning our kids into criminals and our communities and schools into war zones."

'NOT THE CLEAVER KIDS'

In a recent *USA Today*/CNN/Gallup poll, 73 percent of respondents said juveniles who commit violent crimes should be treated as adults. Only 19 percent clearly favored treating juvenile offenders more leniently. Similarly, an NBC/*Wall Street Journal* poll found that 57 percent of respondents thought prosecuting juveniles as young as 14 as adults would make a major difference in reducing crime.

Behind the public's support for such changes, experts say, is outrage fueled by media reports of hard-core, frightening juvenile offenders who have been released back onto the streets.

Typical is the story of Craig Price, a Rhode Island juvenile-training-school inmate, featured on a Jan. 25 segment of the "Dateline NBC" television news magazine. Price, who was arrested at age 15 for the brutal slaying of a Warwick, R.I., woman and her two children, soon confessed to killing a neighbor two years earlier by stabbing her 58 times. An adult convicted of such offenses would likely serve life without parole, but Price, being a juvenile, was sent to juvenile-training center until his 21st birthday.

The Price case has prompted Rhode Island to change its law to allow violent offenders of any age to be tried as adults. So far, though, the state has been unable to block Price's release, and because his juvenile records are sealed, nothing about his deeds would show up on a criminal background check. "Dateline NBC" quoted a local police officer as saying, "There's no doubt in anybody's mind that Craig Price is going to kill again."

These are not the Cleaver kids soaping up some windows...

In delivering their annual addresses, many governors invoked images of cold-blooded teenage killers and noted that children are being arrested for serious crimes at younger ages.

"These are not the Cleaver kids soaping up some windows," Governor Miller said. "These are middle school kids conspiring to hurt their teacher, teenagers shooting people and committing rapes, young thugs running gangs and terrorizing neighborhoods and showing no remorse when they get caught."

According to statistics recently published by the U.S. Justice Department's office of juvenile justice and delinquency prevention, juvenile arrests for violent crimes increased by 50 percent—double the adult increase—between 1987 and 1991. Juvenile arrests for murder rose 85 percent, four times the increase for adults. By the end of that period, juvenile arrests for murder, forcible rape, robbery, and other violent crimes had reached an all-time high and accounted for 17 percent of all arrests for such crimes.

The juvenile-justice office also notes, however, that only 5 percent of juvenile arrests are for violent offenses, and a small proportion of juvenile offenders commit most of the violent and serious crime.

"It is important to emphasize that even though violent juveniles consume the headlines, the actual juvenile offender in most courts is typically a misdemeanor shoplifter. And if they are charged with a felony, it is typically either a burglary or a stolen car," says the University of Minnesota's Feld, who has devoted much of his career to studying juvenile justice.

As the National Center for Juvenile Justice points out, adults still commit more than 90 percent of homicides.

The actual juvenile offender in most courts is typically a misdemeanor shoplifter.

"I think the public is unfairly or inaccurately blaming the youth sector of our population for the increase in violent crime," says Robert E. DeComo, a senior program manager at the National Council on Crime and Delinquency, a non-profit research and consulting organization in San Francisco.

Most of the statutory changes now under consideration call for juveniles to be prosecuted as adults for murder, forcible rape, aggravated assault, and other violent offenses. Several, however, also target juvenile criminals who use guns, sell drugs, or belong to gangs.

SAFETY IN SCHOOLS

If the laws do make a dent in violent juvenile crime, those most likely to be made safer are juveniles themselves. According to the Justice Department's juvenile-justice office, three of every 10 juvenile murder arrests involves a victim under the age of 18. National surveys also have shown that people under the age of 20 account for a disproportionate percentage of violent-crime victims and that teenage victimizations are most likely to occur at school.

Organizations specifically concerned with school safety welcome such proposals. They say the statutory changes would likely improve student discipline and provide more access to information about student crime—information that will enable them to provide young offenders with the supervision and help they need.

Stephens of the National School Safety Center says the use of such laws "will have the effect of warehousing these kids and keeping them out of circulation for a long time." Such an outcome, he maintains, is greatly preferable to the current situation in most communities, where "youngsters who have committed violent offenses, including murder, are being sent back into the public schools as a condition of probation by the juvenile courts."

The current juvenile-justice system "has become a laughing-stock of these kids," says James Corbin, the president of the National Association of School Resource Officers, a nonprofit organization of about 900 certified law-enforcement officers who work in educational settings. "If people believed they would really be punished for bringing weapons and drugs into the schools, there wouldn't be as much of it. Large numbers of these kids have been there four, five, six, or 10 times, and the fear of arrest is nonexistent."

> If people believed they would really be punished for bringing weapons and drugs into the schools, there wouldn't be as much of it.

Glenda Hatchett Johnson, the chief presiding judge of the Fulton County, Ga., juvenile court, points to the tendency for adult courts to hold children for longer periods of time and to make no effort, as juvenile courts do, to promptly return them to school. In doing so, she says, adult courts are more disruptive to the learning process.

Richard J. Fitzgerald, a family-court judge in Louisville, Ky., says another factor can complicate matters even further. Schools are most likely, he maintains, to see such charges leveled against students in classes for the mentally retarded, emotionally disturbed, or learning-disabled.

CODDLE OR CRACK DOWN?

The National Council of Juvenile and Family Court Judges agrees that some children be waived to adult courts. It maintains, however, that juvenile court judges should make such decisions on a case-by-case basis.

James M. Farris, a Beaumont, Tex., juvenile-court judge who serves as the organization's president, contends that research belies the assumption that juvenile courts impose fewer sanctions or give lighter sentences to violent and repeat offenders.

Judge Edwards of the Santa Clara County juvenile court agrees. In fact, he has found that adult courts tend to treat children more lightly because they regard juveniles as first offenders. DeComo of the National Council on Crime and Delinquency adds that prosecutors in the adult-justice system often downgrade the charges leveled against juveniles so they will not fall under mandatory-waiver provisions.

Others question whether the threat of being prosecuted as an adult actually deters juveniles from crime. Children, Judge Fitzgerald asserts, "don't necessary see a linkage between their behaviors and consequences and are not capable of making legal and right decisions without some guidance and structure in their lives."

Seven people around the country have been executed for crimes they committed at the age of 17.

Still other experts raise the most vexing question of all. Hurst of the National Center for Juvenile Justice put it this way in a recent N.C.J.J. newsletter: "If adults commit most of the violence in the country and they are not deterred or corrected by the criminal-justice system, why do we think the criminal-justice system will be effective with juveniles?"

NOT TOO YOUNG TO DIE

Ultimately, experts wonder how the federal and state governments, which are already dealing with widespread overcrowding in the prison system, will find the room and resources to incarcerate large numbers of young criminals. They also question how the courts, and society, will cope with the more troubling consequences of the new laws.

As a result of its waivers, inmates who committed crimes as juveniles are showing up on Florida's death row. One of them is Jeffrey Farina. He shot three people and stabbed another in a fast-food store in 1992; one victim died. Asked why he did it, Farina said simply, "I had a boring day."

More than a dozen states currently place no age restrictions on those who can be sentenced to death for capital crimes. Over the past two decades, seven people around the country have been executed for crimes they committed at the age of 17. In 1989, the U.S. Supreme Court upheld the death sentence of a 16-year old murderer. The year before, however, the Court blocked the execution of a 15-year-old on grounds it would violate the Constitution's prohibition against cruel and unusual punishment.

Prisons and jails also will have to deal with the fact that juvenile inmates who are not placed in separate facilities will be vulnerable to victimization by their fellow prisoners. Governor Miller of Georgia has proposed establishing a separate correctional facility for juveniles tried as adults, but most states plan to continue to house them in regular jails and prisons.

"Look, these kids are all going to be coming back to society," says the University of Minnesota's Feld. "We need to think about what they are going to be like when they come back."

Okaying the Use of Metal Detectors Proves Easier Than Actually Using Them

by Philip Stelly

I n an effort to stop violence in the New Orleans Public Schools, the Orleans Parish school board has authorized the use of metal detectors to ferret out guns and other weapons. The detectors now are in place and authorized, but a controversy over the devices so far has prevented them from being used.

The board's metal detector policy says teachers, administrators, and school security officials may use hand-held metal detectors to search students suspected of carrying concealed weapons in schools or at events such as football and basketball games. The push for the policy came after the school board was presented with evidence that at least 87 incidents involving metal weapons (as well as some nonmetal weapons) had occurred during the 1981-82 school year. Those incidents included altercations resulting in the deaths of a student and a former student.

The issue of how and when metal detectors could be used came to the board's attention after it learned that A. C. Boyd, director of security for the schools and a former official of the Federal Bureau of Investigation, had purchased the security devices. When the board found that at least 15 school principals had requested the detectors, the school board set to work formulating a policy on the matter.

The policy the board finally adopted is a compromise: Board Member John Robbert had proposed that the school sys-

From *The American School Board Journal,* vol. 171, no. 3, p. 47, March 1984. Reprinted with permission.

tem adopt a measure that would include wholesale searches of students and anyone else attending a school-sponsored activity. Citing the use of metal detection devices at airports and in federal buildings, Robbert said wholesale searches wouldn't discriminate against individuals and would be preferable to asking school personnel to pick out specific students for the searches. He argued that the wholesale searches would be acceptable if prior notice were given that the hand-held devices were to be used at school functions. A group of black citizens and the American Civil Liberties Union (A.C.L.U.) objected, claiming that a student's Fourth Amendment protection against unreasonable search and seizure would be violated by Robbert's proposed policy. But the A.C.L.U. did support an alternate policy that would allow selective use of the wand-like metal detectors in specific circumstances that were spelled out clearly. Selective use, the A.C.L.U. said, would be less intrusive than physical frisking of suspected students by school personnel.

> As effective as the metal detectors might be in keeping weapons off school grounds, board members admit that the devices are only a stopgap.

Before adopting a final policy, the school board asked for the opinion of School Board Attorney Charles T. Curtis, Jr., who stated, "Generally, rather than having to prove probable cause, schools need only show that there was 'reasonable suspicion' or a 'reasonable cause to believe' that a school rule or state law was being violated to validate a search of a student's person or belongings." On this advice, the board adopted a policy that says the hand-held metal detector *may* be used to search a student "where a school official has articulable facts which lead to a reasonable belief" that the student possesses a weapon or illegal drug.

As effective as the metal detectors might be in keeping weapons off school grounds, board members admit that the devices are only a stopgap; long-range solutions will have to be discovered and implemented later. A task force has been formed to investigate the issues of building and equipment security, transportation safety, and student security in the school system. One goal of the task force, say school board spokesmen, is to dispel the myth that schools are a breeding ground for violence.

The task force will call on community leaders to help find ways to promote school security.

In spite of the board policy, the principals who originally called for the devices have become reluctant to use the metal detectors. "School principals are caught in the middle," says Kenneth J. DuCote, director of planning for the school system. "They are afraid that if someone gets killed in one of their schools, the principal will be called into court to explain why a detector was not used. But if they do use the metal detectors, they are afraid they might get pulled before a judge and accused of violating student rights."

Confronting the Crisis in the Criminal Justice System

by Sara Podell

America has a crime problem and an overwhelming drug problem. The result is overburdened courts, overworked prosecutors and defense attorneys, and insufficient prison space. The American public recognizes these individual realities, but what it may not recognize is that these facts together have produced a crisis in the criminal justice system. Experts from diverse fields have examined this crisis, both its components and its whole. However, their analyses of its sources, consequences, and solutions often diverge.

> **A quick fix is particularly unlikely to solve the complex problems of the criminal justice system.**

DOES THE BILL OF RIGHTS UNDERMINE THE CRIMINAL JUSTICE SYSTEM?

In looking at any problem, the natural tendency is to pinpoint one particular cause and fix it. While attractive, this type of approach is always dangerous. Quick fixes usually don't work, and a quick fix is particularly unlikely to solve the complex problems of the criminal justice system.

In 1986, the American Bar Association Section on Criminal Justice created a committee to examine how well the criminal justice system was working and to identify how to improve it. The Special Committee on Criminal Justice in a Free Society was chaired by Samuel Dash, former Philadelphia district attorney and a former chairperson of the ABA Criminal Justice Section, who is perhaps best known for his service as chief counsel

From *Technical Assistance Bulletin*, no. 5, published by the American Bar Association. Reprinted with permission.

to the Senate Watergate Committee. He is now a law professor at Georgetown University in Washington, DC. The committee produced a report, *Criminal Justice in Crisis,* which carefully examined the perception that the individual protections of the Fourth, Fifth, and Sixth Amendments to the Constitution prevent the criminal justice system from functioning properly.

By surveying police chiefs, district attorneys, defense attorneys and judges—the people at the "front lines"—the committee concluded that constitutional guarantees are not handcuffing law enforcement. It emphasized the grave error of scapegoating constitutional protections and scrapping them as part of a "get tough on crime" program. A police lieutenant explains, for example, that the *Miranda* warnings are "a routine [Arrestees have] been through it. We've been through it. . . . It doesn't, frankly, interfere too much with confessions, surprisingly enough." (*Criminal Justice in Crisis,* pp. 28–29) A trial judge states, "It's very rare that confessions are kicked out in court. . . . Essentially, I think that the Fourth and Fifth Amendments have really made the police officers better police officers because they have to be smarter police officers." A prosecuting attorney concurs, explaining that a "good police officers [could talk defendants into confessing before or after] there was a *Miranda.* . . . and so [the decision] had no real impact at all upon the ability of good police officers to get confessions." (*Criminal Justice in Crisis,* p. 31)

> [Some] politicians use the Bill of Rights as a scapegoat for their own failure to address the crime problem honestly.

Dash and Sharon Goretsky, a consultant to the ABA Section of Criminal Justice, comment that "[some] politicians use the Bill of Rights as a scapegoat for their own failure to address the crime problem honestly. (Dash and Goretsky, "We Don't Need to Give Up Our Constitutional Protections," *Criminal Justice,* Vol. 5, No. 1, p. 3) Dash, Goretsky and many other analysts are careful to point out that the crucial task is to face the crime problem in all its complexity. Convincing the American public that sacrificing their constitutional protections will save the system can only make situations worse. "Out of 34 million serious felonies . . . in 1985, 31 million never got into the criminal justice system because they were unreported, or if reported, they remained unsolved." (Dash and Goretsky, p. 3) If, as these figures indicate, 90% of felonies never enter the system at all, the Fourth, Fifth and Sixth Amendments' protection of individuals at the time of arrest and during trials could hardly be the major source of the system's failings. What, then, are the major sources?

CONFRONTING THE DRUG PROBLEM

Most analysts agree that one of the greatest challenges facing the criminal justice system is the nation's overwhelming drug problem. They also agree that not only do politicians and the public need to recognize that the drug problem cannot be addressed by law enforcement alone, but they must be willing to put forth money for a comprehensive program which includes treatment and education.

How much attention should be devoted to law enforcement solutions? How should funding be divided between law enforcement and treatment and education? Should more money be invested in law enforcement? These are the hotly debated questions.

> The drug problem in this country is severe, growing worse, and... law enforcement has been unable to control the problem.

At both the national and local levels, governments are pouring a great deal of money into law enforcement. The findings of the Special Committee on Criminal Justice in a Free Society show that despite this high level of funding, "the drug problem in this country is severe, growing worse, and . . . law enforcement has been unable to control the problem." (*Criminal Justice in Crisis*, p. 44) A police lieutenant quoted in the committee's report comments: "There is no law enforcement solution to the problem. . . . It is ultimately a social problem." (*Criminal Justice in Crisis*, p. 45) Dash and Goretsky add that "the President's current war on drugs simply will not work and will only to lead to more public disappointment, anger and frustration." (Dash and Goretsky, p. 4) While encouraged by President Bush's recognition that law enforcement alone cannot remedy the problem, they note that the President still allots only a small portion of available funds to education, treatment and other non-law enforcement programs.

Judge Reggie B. Walton, on the other hand, believes that the President's program is on the right track to solving the drug crisis. Judge Walton is associate director of the Office of National Drug Control Policy of the Executive Office of the President. He stresses that the President believes that education is the ultimate tool to overcoming this problem. Towards that goal, he says, the President has recommended that funding for drug education programs be increased by $37 million. He also states, "We will seek to beef up our law enforcement efforts so that we can go after more people and make them accountable for their illegal conduct." (Walton, "Why We Need to Win the War Against Drugs," *Update on Law-Related Education,* Winter 1990, p. 4)

THE WORD ON THE STREET

There are similar disagreements on the local level as to how much money should be allocated to law enforcement's role in combating the drug problem. New York City is a prime example of how the push for more drug arrests has clogged cities' criminal justice systems. An April 1989 article in the *New York Times* stated that "The root of the crisis, many officials assert, was a decision last year by the Koch administration to allocate $116 million over two years for the politically popular Tactical Narcotics Teams (TNT), special teams intended to saturate designated areas and street level arrests." (Pitt, "Drug Cases Clog New York City Courts," *New York Times,* April 4, 1989, p. 24) Of this $116 million, $9.5 million—slightly more than 8%—was budgeted for the Legal Aid Society and the district attorneys.

However, district attorneys working in the TNT areas said this money would still be insufficient to cover the costs of dealing with the increasing number of felony drug cases. Most New York lawyers, judges and police agree that the city's system is so bogged down that many traffickers and users will end up back on the streets because there are not enough people or funds to process them. "I've been told by some [New York] judges, explains Samuel Dash, "that if someone charged with a felony jumps bail and doesn't show up in court they all celebrate and applaud." (Dash, "Can the Bill of Rights Survive the Crisis in Criminal Justice?" *Update on Law-Related Education*, Winter 1990, p. 9) And while the situation in New York may be severe, Manhattan District Attorney Robert Morgenthau reports that it's even worse in Miami, Los Angeles and Washington, DC.

Those who advocate a "get tough" policy on the streets believe that this is the best way to send the message that the government is serious about winning the war on drugs. Their opponents believe that massive arrests will be useless if the system is unable to process the suspects. Chief Judge Sol Wachtler emphasizes that "what is being lost is the certainty of punishment, which is even more important as a deterrent to crime than the severity." (Pitt, p. 24) An additional and often overlooked consequence is the demoralizing effect this "revolving door" has on police who must watch helplessly as suspects are returned to the streets.

> To most drug dealers the prospect of making millions far outstrips the risk of a three-year prison sentence with a chance of parole in 18 months.

Richard Abell, former assistant attorney general in charge of the Office of Justice Programs, takes a contrary view. He stresses that "to most drug dealers the prospect of making millions far outstrips the risk of a three-year prison sentence with a chance of parole in 18 months. A 15-year mandatory sentence with no chance of parole would send a dramatically different message." (Abell, "The Costly Crisis in Corrections," the *Wall Street Journal*, March 21, 1989, p. A26)

Whether one chooses to stress certainty or severity of punishment to deter crime, suspects have the right to a trial. If they are convicted and sentenced to prison, there must be room for them in prison. This seems obvious, but the system is currently so starved for resources and personnel, and the prisons are so overcrowded, that vigorous law enforcement might cause the system to collapse before it could affect the drug trade.

THE SYSTEM'S IMBALANCE

Regardless of one's position on the issue, one fact is inescapable: a lack of funds has weakened the justice system. In New York

City, for example, the TNT allocation was made "without seeking a commensurate rise in state and city funds for the courts, the district attorneys, the city's Correction and Probation Departments, the Legal Aid Society and drug treatment centers and education programs." (Pitt, p. 24) Former Chief Justice Burger warned against this kind of imbalance when he compared the criminal trial process to a three-legged stool comprised of the judge, the prosecutor and the defense attorney. "The weakness of any one of the legs," he said, "will cause the process to tumble." (Dash and Goretsky, p. 4)

One example of this can be seen in the current use of plea negotiation. According to information collected by the Special Committee on Criminal Justice in a Free Society, plea bargaining is widely distrusted by the public. Although plea bargaining might strengthen the justice system under certain conditions, justice officials repeatedly told the committee that now "plea negotiation was essential because the system simply could not function if more defendants exercised the right to trial." (*Criminal Justice in Crisis*, p. 41) Thus there is a pressure to negotiate pleas even though this practice may not be in the best interest of either the public or the defendant.

In addition, the committee found that public defense services are plummeting in quality because the attorneys must take on more cases than they can handle. Prosecutors face the same problem. "We're swamped," explains Brooklyn District Attorney Elizabeth Holtzman. "We've got assistant district attorneys handling 120 cases each and Criminal Court judges dealing with 250 to 400 cases apiece." (Pitt, p. 24) Because of the number of cases on court dockets, suspects often must wait to be arraigned three to four times longer than they did in the past.

PRISON CROWDING

In view of the prison system's widely acknowledged problems, many question the strategy of fighting drug crimes with longer prison sentences. As American Bar Association President Jack Curtin observes, "[O]ur jails and prisons are bursting at the seams. Forty states are under court order for unconstitutional conditions in their correctional facilities." In many jurisdictions, Curtin notes, crowding is exacerbated by sentencing mandates which force judges to send first offenders, especially first-time drug offenders, to prison.

While new prisons are being built at an unprecedented rate—and at astronomical costs of between $50,000 and $100,000 per bed—new construction cannot keep pace with the rising rate of incarceration. Since 1970, the number of persons in state and federal prisons has tripled. A report from The Sentencing Project in Washington, DC indicates that the United States has the highest incarceration rate in the world.

> While new prisons are being built at an unprecedented rate...new construction cannot keep pace with the rising rate of incarceration.

One way to alleviate the crisis, according to some analysts, is through prison privatization. Under this arrangement, the government contracts with a private company to house and monitor prisoners. Private companies can often build and run prisons for less than the government, and still make a profit. Several such prisons have already been established in Texas, Kentucky and New Mexico.

Some question, however, whether saving money justifies handing over governmental responsibility for prisoners to a private entity. Edward Koren of the National Prison Project of the American Civil Liberties Union comments that the governments may not "always have the best interest of prisoners at heart, but at least they're accountable to the people. Who holds these companies accountable?" (Belkin, "Rise of Private Prisons: How Much of a Bargain?," *New York Times*, March 27, 1989, p. 8) The ability of the government to ensure the constitutional rights of prisoners in such facilities is a central issue in this debate.

One consequence of overcrowding, according to *Criminal Justice in Crisis*, is that parole boards are forced to release offenders too soon. "An inmate who serves 40% of his sentence has served a lot of time...[I]f the public is upset, they are going to have to address the governor or the state authorities." (*Criminal Justice in Crisis*, p. 43) This type of request for support and action by the public is echoed by many of the people surveyed in all areas of the criminal justice system.

WHAT THE PUBLIC CAN DO

Many observers believe that the public must first come to understand that the criminal justice system has a limited role in reducing crime. People must begin to see that the crime problem, whether related to drugs or not, is a societal problem that has its roots in both economic status imbalance and a weakened moral system. A Washington DC high school student reacting to President Bush's "Say No to Drugs" speech said, "I make a hundred bucks an hour selling drugs. What does the President want me to do, work at McDonald's for the minimum wage?" (Dash, p. 9) "The public," says Dash, "unfortunately believes that if the police worked honestly and competently they would protect them against crime. . . . It's impossible. It's impossible for the policeman on the street to solve the crime problem." (Dash, p. 8) When the public accepts this fact, perhaps it will realize that it can make important contributions to fighting the crime problem.

For example, communities can establish task forces to address the problems the criminal justice system faces and set priorities for government spending. Citizens can mobilize to demand greater funding for education, treatment, and the courts. Because much crime in America is committed by youth, many of those surveyed in *Criminal Justice in Crisis* emphasized their belief that "providing services for neglected, abused, and delinquent youth could have a significant impact on the incidence of crime." (*Criminal Justice in Crisis*, p. 53)

Educators also have an important role. They can invite judges, attorneys, legislators and justice system professionals to speak to students about the myths and realities of the criminal justice system. They can serve as crucial liaisons between the system and the community. Almost every analyst stresses that there is fragmentation not only within the system itself, but also in the relationship between the system and the nation it serves. Communication, therefore, is a vital first step towards establishing a foundation of knowledge upon which effective, lasting and just solutions can be built.

We Need a National Strategy for Safe Schools

by Gus Frias

Educators and community leaders must learn how to work together in a dangerous world.

The sixth of our National Education Goals calls for every school in America to be free of drugs and violence by the year 2000 and to offer a disciplined environment conducive to learning. The new Safe Schools Act allocates $20 million to this effort in the form of 20 one-year grants, intended to reinforce existing school safety programs.

> **Every school administrator has a duty to protect the health and safety of his students and staff.**

As a 15-year veteran of efforts to prevent gang violence and create safe schools in southern California, I find the current legislation myopic and unrealistic. If we are truly serious about Goal Number 6—if we are not just mouthing fine-sounding words—we must have a national strategy that creates a shared vision, includes every state (not just 20), and provides clear guidelines for safety initiatives at the individual school level. Such a strategy should include, at a minimum, three components:

1. REQUIRE THE CREATION OF COMPREHENSIVE SCHOOL SAFETY PLANS AT ALL PUBLIC SCHOOLS.

Every school administrator has a duty to protect the health and safety of his students and staff. An effective school safety plan includes the following elements:

From *The Harvard Education Newsletter*, vol. X, no. 3, p. 4–5, May/June 1994. Reprinted with permission.

- **Establish an interagency safe-school team at each site.** Start by identifying a group of highly committed individuals. The purpose of this team is to share responsibility and accountability for assessing risks and for planning, implementing, coordinating, and evaluating violence prevention efforts. Each team should have an administrator, a teacher, a parent, two students, the head custodian, a local business person, and a police officer.

> The school safety plan must start with clear, realistic, and measurable goals.

- **Create a violence prevention vision.** Unity of vision is necessary for sacrifice and for action. This vision must be multi-disciplinary in the interrelated areas of suppression, intervention, and prevention.

- **Establish goals and objectives.** The school safety plan must start with clear, realistic, and measurable goals to address the emotional, spiritual, and physical needs of students and their families. For example, older students can be trained to mentor younger ones on coping with pain and adversity at home and at school. The goal that every student should either be or have a mentor can be stated and the results tracked.

- **Create a detailed plan of action.** Delegate duties and responsibilities to each team member with specific timelines for completion.

- **Train teachers.** All educators need to know what is expected of them in preventing and responding to school crime and violence. Training should emphasize protective strategies and include crisis management and cultural awareness activities, where appropriate.

- **Educate parents.** All parents should be taught ways they can help prevent violence and recognize early indicators of drug abuse and gang activity. They need to know how the law applies to them and their children and what resources are available in the school and community to support them.

- **Develop student leadership.** Create a leadership class that meets daily for 25 of the school's most influential students. Half should be from the group considered to be at high risk. The purpose is to nurture a cadre of responsible students who will assist in violence prevention work.

• **Adopt a violence prevention curriculum.** Include the teaching of responsible citizenship, the strength of cultural diversity, choices and consequences, and conflict resolution skills. A good curriculum is incremental, age-appropriate, culturally sensitive, teacher-friendly, and consistent with other home and community initiatives. Most important, it should be integrated into the school's existing curriculum framework.

• **Prepare for crises.** Examine all existing plans for responding to a crisis. Analyze real-life cases. Identify a team of responders with clearly defined duties and roles. Conduct a crisis drill, evaluate the results, and modify the plans. This part of the plan should be directed by the team's law-enforcement representative.

• **Offer after-school activities for students.** These should include both recreation and tutoring. Provide mentors to help students with homework and to organize sports. Keep the school grounds open until 8 p.m.

• **Create school-business partnerships.** These can be sources of both after-school mentors and employment apprenticeship programs for students and their families.

• **Build a strong interagency team structure.** Review the team's expectations and limitations and discuss ways to adapt them. Create memorandums of understanding and seek court orders, if necessary, to facilitate the sharing of confidential information about crime and violence on or near school grounds.

2. REMOVE A SCHOOL'S IMMUNITY IF ADMINISTRATORS FAIL TO CREATE A SCHOOL SAFETY PLAN.

Many schools currently rely on the presence of just one police officer to address school safety. Therefore, if a violent incident occurs and that officer is not available, the school is unprepared. Other schools offer semi-annual one-hour violence prevention assemblies for teachers, students, and parents. These serve little purpose but to limit the school's legal liability in case of a violent incident. At some schools, administrators are still in a state of total denial and take no action at all.

School officials must be compelled to take their duty of care and responsibility seriously. If a child or teacher is killed on school grounds and no safety plan was in place, "I'm sorry" is simply not good enough. We must enforce a higher standard, including holding officials legally liable when they fail to adopt comprehensive school safety plans.

3. CREATE A NATIONAL TEAM-TRAINING ACADEMY.
Educators and community leaders alike need help in learning how to work together. Interagency personnel, in particular, face enormous barriers rooted in egoistic, territorial, and distrustful thinking. A national academy for training violence prevention teams could help us understand each other's strengths and weaknesses and learn to trust each other.

Exercising leadership in a violent environment is dangerous. We must learn the lessons of the past to avoid making deadly errors. The world does not need martyrs. It needs living heroes and heroines who can teach young people to reject violent, self-destructive behavior and to embrace life, education, family, and community. Making this happen will require brains, faith, and courage.

Honorable Mention: Agencies, Bureaus, and Coalitions

In the past, schools have been used to solve social problems. Unfortunately, schools are blamed when the social problems don't get solved immediately. Educators do not need to receive more blame for the ills of today. Instead, the general public needs to realize that the causes and problems of violence cannot be solved solely in school. Solutions will be found when parents, students, and educators work together with the judicial and enforcement agencies, public health, and other social service providers. Educators cannot afford to let the public "off the hook" by assuming all of the responsibility. Only a team effort will solve a problem of this magnitude.

Section Four offers a wealth of resources for creating innovative ways of working with troubled youth. The list is not exhaustive, but it does represent a wide range of agencies that are attempting to deal with violence problems. Many offer helpful programs and curriculum materials. These valuable resources were found in the SouthEastern Regional Vision for Education's book, *Hot Topics: Usable Research, Reducing School Violence.*

Annotated Resources

by Stephanie Kadel and Joseph Follman

T he following list of organizations, publications, and curricula can be used by districts and schools working to reduce school violence. Some of the information and services
are offered at no cost; others require payment. Many of the
organizations offer useful publications which are described
briefly. Note: the description of organizations and publications
in this document does not imply an endorsement by SERVE.

ORGANIZATIONS
The American-Arab Anti-Discrimination Committee
4201 Connecticut Ave., NW
Suite 500
Washington, DC 20008
(202) 244-2990
The ADC is a civil rights organization devoted to the elimination
of discrimination against Arabs and Arab-Americans. It collects
and disseminates statistics on Anti-Arab hate crime and maintains
a legal services division.

American Bar Association
Special Committee on Dispute Resolution
1800 M Street, NW
Washington, DC 20036
(202) 331-2258
The ABA committee acts as a clearinghouse in the field of school
mediation and publishes the *Directory to School Mediation Projects*
which is available to schools.

From *Hot Topics: Usable Research, Reducing School Violence*, the SouthEastern
Regional Vision for Education, 1993, p. 67–69. Reprinted with permission.

American Jewish Committee
Institute of Human Relations
165 East 56th Street
New York, NY 10022
(212) 751-4000
The AJC was established in 1906 as a human relations organization
to protect the safety and security of Jews everywhere. Since then, it
has expanded its scope to include activities that safeguard the human rights of all American citizens. Forty chapters exist around the
U.S. They have developed conflict resolution programs such as
"Ethnic Sharing" for use by schools and other institutions.

Boys and Girls Clubs of America
611 Rockville Pike, Suite 230
Rockville, MD 20852
(301) 251-6676
This national nonprofit youth organization provides support services to 1,240 Boys and Girls Club facilities that help over 1.6 million young people nationwide connect with opportunities for personal growth and achievement. It is the only major nationwide
youth agency with a primary mission of service to disadvantaged
girls and boys.

Bureau of Alcohol, Tobacco and Firearms
U.S. Treasury Department
650 Massachusetts Ave., NW
Washington, DC 20226
(202) 927-7777
BATF operates a hotline, 800-ATF-GUNS, that individuals can call
to report possible firearms and drug or gang activity and other
crimes. Agents staffing the hotline share the tips with local, state,
and federal law enforcement agencies.

Bureau of Justice Assistance Clearinghouse
Box 6000
Rockville, MD 20850
(800) 688-4252
This clearinghouse provides information and publications on BJA-
funded anti-crime and anti-drug programs, including formula
grants, technical assistance, training, and demonstration projects.
Seven federal clearinghouses can be reached by calling (800) 788-

2800. Of special interest to educators are the National Clearing-house for Alcohol and Drug Information, the Drugs and Crime Data Center, the Drug Abuse Information and Referral Hotline, the Drug Information Strategy Clearinghouse, and the National Criminal Justice Reference Service.

Center for Democratic Renewal
Post Office Box 50469
Atlanta, GA 30302
(404) 221-0025
The Center is a national civil rights organization that monitors white supremacists and far right activities. It also helps communities in combating hate violence.

Center to Prevent Handgun Violence
1225 I Street, NW
Suite 1150
Washington, DC 20005
(202) 289-7319
This organization provides educational materials and programs for adults and children on preventing gun deaths and injuries. It offers information about children and gun violence, firearm homicide, suicide, and unintentional shootings, violence in schools, black-on-black violence, and conflict resolution.

Children's Creative Response to Conflict
Box 271
523 North Broadway
Nyack, NY 10960
(914) 358-4601
CCRC offers workshops in creative conflict resolution for children and people who work with children, emphasizing themes of cooperation, communication, affirmation (building self-esteem), and conflict resolution. They also publish a source book of activities, *The Friendly Classroom for a Small Planet.*

Intercultural Communication Institute
8835 Southwest Canyon Lane
Suite 238
Portland, OR 97225
(503) 297-4622

The Intercultural Communication Institute is a nonprofit organization designed to foster an awareness and appreciation of cultural differences. The Institute is based on the belief that education and training in intercultural communication will improve competence in dealing with cultural diversity and minimize destructive conflicts among national, cultural, and ethnic groups. It provides technical assistance to schools and groups on a variety of topics related to intergroup relations.

Kids + Guns = A Deadly Equation
1450 Northeast 2nd Avenue
Room 523A
Miami, FL 33132
(305) 995-1986
This program is designed to teach young children the dangers of playing with or carrying weapons. School-based, the program helps K-12 students learn to avoid weapons.

Klanwatch Project
Southern Poverty Law Center
400 Washington Avenue
Montgomery, AL 36104
(205) 264-0286
The Southern Poverty Law Center, founded in 1971, is a nonprofit foundation supported by private donations. The Center's Klanwatch Project was formed in 1980 to help curb Klu Klux Klan and racist violence through litigation, education, and monitoring. Since 1980, lawsuits brought by SPLC and Klanwatch have resulted in federal civil rights indictments against numerous hate groups around the nation.

Male Health Alliance for Life Extension
10 Sunnybrook Road
Post Office Box 1409
Raleigh, NC 27620
(919) 250-4535
The MHALE program targets at-risk African-American males aged 11–17 and provides life skills training, vocational education and counseling, conflict-resolution training, and remedial basic education.

National Association for Mediation in Education
425 Amity Street
Amherst, MA 01002
(413) 545-2462
NAME is a national clearinghouse for information about conflict-resolution programs in schools.

National Institute Against Prejudice and Violence
710 Lombard Street
Baltimore, MD 21201
(410) 706-5170
The purpose of the Institute is to study and respond to the problem of violence and intimidation motivated by racial, religious, ethnic, or anti-gay prejudice. Activities include collecting, analyzing, producing, and disseminating information and materials on programs of prevention and response. The Institute conducts research on the causes and prevalence of prejudice and violence and their effects on victims and society; provides technical assistance to public agencies, voluntary organizations, schools, and communities in conflict; analyzes and drafts model legislation; conducts educational and training programs; and sponsors conferences, symposia, and other forums for information exchange among experts.

National Institute for Dispute Resolution
1901 L Street, NW, Suite 600
Washington, DC 20036
(202) 466-4764
This organization works to enhance the understanding, acceptance, and development of a spectrum of tools to resolve conflict, including mediation, arbitration, and negotiation. Among its current grant programs and initiatives are Mediation in Schools, Community-Based Dispute Resolution Centers, Court-Based Dispute Resolution Programs, and Statewide Offices of Mediation.

National Victims Resource Center
Box 6000-AJE
Rockville, MD 20850
(800) 627-6872 or
(301) 251-5525/5519

The NVRC is a national clearinghouse for victims' information funded by the Office for Victims of Crime, U.S. Department of Justice. The NVRC is one of several information resources maintained by the National Criminal Justice Reference Service. Information specialists at the NVRC have access to a database that indexes more than 7,000 victim-related books and articles with information on child physical and sexual abuse, victims' services, domestic violence, victim-witness programs, and violent crime.

Project RAP (Reaching Adulthood Prepared)
380 Timothy Road
Athens, GA 30606
(706) 549-1435
Project RAP is a mentoring program for black youth aged 12–17 which uses church and community volunteers as role models and mentors.

Violence Intervention Program
Durham Public Schools
Post Box 30002
Durham, NC 27702
(919) 560-2035
Designed to help at-risk elementary school children, the VIP program pairs children with teachers who help them with conflict mediation and resolution skills and also serve as peer counselors and tutors.

Violence Prevention Program
Mecklenburg County Health Department
249 Billingsley Road
Charlotte, NC 28211
(704) 336-5497
This county program teaches conflict resolution skills to seventh through ninth graders and serves as a support group for the youth.

YES! Atlanta
955 Spring Street
Atlanta, GA 30309
(404) 874-6996
This project provides mentoring, tutoring, and job skills training to youth aged 13 to 18 who live in housing projects.

The Youth Gang Drug Prevention Program
Mecklenburg County Health Department
249 Billingsley Road
Charlotte, NC 28211
(704) 336-6443
Designed to help steer youth ages 10–18 away from gang membership, this program sponsors recreation activities and education in conflict resolution for youth and their families.

Publications, Guidebooks, and Curricula

by Stephanie Kadel and Joseph Follman

Alternatives to Suspension by the Florida Department of Education, 1991. This publication offers many alternatives to out-of-school suspension and expulsion and examines how schools can take steps to reduce overall school violence. Published by the Center for Prevention and Student Assistance, Florida Department of Education, Room 414 Florida Education Center, 325 West Gaines Street, Tallahassee, FL 32399-0400 (904) 488-6315.

Alternatives to Violence curriculum by Peace Grows, Inc. Peace Grows publishes several curriculum guides and other publications designed to reduce youth violence through mediation. The organization also offers a number of training packages, ranging from four to forty hours in length. Publications and training examine violence at all levels—from the interpersonal to the international—are aimed at promoting pacifism, and contain useful activities for high school students. Published by Peace Grows, Inc., 513 W. Exchange Street, Akron, OH 44302 (216) 864-5442.

Anger: The Misunderstood Emotion by Carol Tarvis, 1982. A witty and highly readable survey of research that challenges nearly all commonly held assumptions about anger. Published by Simon and Schuster, New York.

Appreciating Differences: Teaching and Learning in a Culturally Diverse Classroom by Evelyn Ploumis-Devick, 1992. This publication, from the SouthEastern Regional Vision for Education *Hot Topics: Usable Research* series, is a practical guidebook for helping teachers infuse their curricula with a multicultural perspective. In addition to descriptions of many exemplary school

From *Hot Topics: Usable Research, Reducing School Violence,* the SouthEastern Regional Vision for Education, 1993, p. 70–72. Reprinted with permission.

programs and lists of resources and contacts, the publication offers several dozen multicultural activities, lessons, games, and projects that can be used with students of various ages. Published by SERVE, 345 S. Magnolia Drive, Suite D-23, Tallahassee, FL 32301-2950 (800) 352-6001.

Celebrating Diversity by D. Powers, 1990. This publication is a presentation manual for conducting a day-long training session in appreciating cultural diversity. Produced by the Equal Education Opportunity Program, Florida Department of Education, Suite 1020, Florida Education Center, 325 West Gaines Street, Tallahassee, FL 32399-0400.

Challenging Racism by D. Powers, 1990. This publication is a presentation manual for conducting a day-long training session on addressing the problem of racism. Produced by the Equal Education Opportunity Program, Florida Department of Education, Suite 1020, Florida Education Center, 325 West Gaines Street, Tallahassee, FL 32399-0400.

Children of War by Roger Rosenblatt, 1983. The author has traveled widely to discover what children in war-torn countries think and feel about the violence around them. The children he interviews shine through as champions of order in the midst of chaos, quietly resistant to adult attempts to use their tragedies as tools of ideology or instruments of revenge. Published by Anchor Press/Doubleday, New York.

Conflict Resolution Curriculum Packet by Tom and Frances Bigda-Peyton. Designed by high school teachers to teach high school students the basics of conflict resolution, this resource clearly demonstrates how conflict-resolution skills can be applied at all levels. Published by Boston-Area Educators for Social Responsibility, 11 Garden Street, Cambridge, MA 02138.

Creative Conflict Resolution: Over 200 Activities for Keeping Peace in the Classroom by William J. Kreidler. Although designed as a guide to conflict resolution in the elementary classroom, this resource contains many activities that can be easily adapted to the high school level. Published by Goodyear Books,

Scott, Foresman and Company, 1900 East Lake Avenue, Glenview, IL 60025.

Cross-Cultural Communication: An Essential Dimension of Effective Education by Orlando Taylor, 1987. Produced by the Mid-Atlantic Center for Race Equity, American University, 5010 Wisconsin Avenue, NW, #310, Washington, DC 20016.

Developing Personal and Social Responsibility: A Guide for Community Action, by D. R. Grossnickle, and R. D. Stephens, 1992. Published by the National School Safety Center, Malibu, California.

Discipline Strategies for Teachers (Fastback #344) by Eleanor Barron, 1992. Intended primarily for student teachers and beginning teachers, this document provides practical strategies for both classroom management and discipline. Theory is illustrated in scenarios using positive and negative examples. Published by Phi Delta Kappa Educational Foundation, Bloomington, Indiana.

Effective Strategies for School Security by P. D. Blauvelt, 1981. Published by the National Association of Secondary School Principals, Reston, Virginia (ERIC Document Reproduction Service No. ED 209 774)

Gang Awareness and Intervention: Activities for Elementary and Middle School Students. Published by the Child Development Specialist Program at the Portland Public Schools, Office of Public Information, P.O. Box 3107, Portland, OR 97222.

Getting to Yes: Negotiating Agreements Without Giving In by Roger Fischer and William Ury, 1981. A fascinating introduction to conflict resolution by two of the field's experts. Published by Houghton Mifflin, Boston.

Guidelines for Policies Addressing Sexual Misconduct Toward Students in Public Schools, 1992. This publication offers clear and direct guidelines for procedures to be adopted to address the concerns surrounding sexual harassment in schools. Overviews of major court cases in the area of sexual harassment in schools are also included as well as a number of newspaper articles on the subject. Published by the Florida Department of Education, PL08, The Capitol, Tallahassee, FL 32399 (904) 487-1785.

Hate Crime: Sourcebook for Schools by C. Bodinger-De Uriarte and A. R. Sancho, 1992. A comprehensive examination of the problem of hate crimes in America, this publication details the roots, nature and scope of the problem and offers practical suggestions for reducing hate crimes. Published by Research for Better Schools, 444 North 3rd Street, Philadelphia, PA 19123.

"Human Relations Education: Teaching Non-Violent Solutions to Human Problems" by Ruth Gudinas, *Forum*, Summer 1987. Gudinas discusses how educators can teach about human conflicts and how the process should expand as children become young adults. She also includes information on how to help children learn about alternatives that they can use to resolve conflict peacefully.

I AM Somebody: A Comprehensive Guide to Educate Youth About the Seriousness of Gang Involvement by Clarence Hill, Gang Consultant (middle and high school levels). Published by the Portland Redirection Program, 1032 North Sumner, Portland, OR 97217.

Interagency Collaboration: Improving the Delivery of Services to Children and Families by Stephanie Kadel, 1992. This publication, from the SERVE *Hot Topics: Usable Research* series, is a practical guidebook for establishing or expanding collaborative efforts to provide services to children and families at a single, easily accessible site such as a school. Many examples are offered of communities and schools that have had success in this effort, and resources and contacts are provided for additional information. Available from SERVE, 345 South Magnolia Drive, Suite D-23, Tallahassee, FL 32301-2950 (800) 352-6001.

Nobody Likes a Bully. Published by the School of Education, Winthrop College, Rock Hill, SC 29733 (803) 323-2151.

Peacemaking by Barbara Stanford, 1976. A comprehensive introduction to conflict resolution by a leading educator in the field. Contains many exercises that can be used with high school students. Published by Bantam Books, New York.

Peer Leader Training Manual—Three Session Curriculum for Teaching Adolescents by C. Sousa, L. Bancroft, & T. German, 1991. Published by the Dating Violence Instruction Project, c/o Transition House, P.O. Box 530, Harvard Square Station, Cambridge, MA 02238.

Preventing Family Violence by the Family Violence Curriculum Project. A comprehensive, useful, and sensitively designed curriculum dealing with such controversial issues as family violence, child sexual abuse, and date rape. Published by Massachusetts Department of Public Health, Resource Center for the Prevention of Family Violence, 150 Tremont Street, Boston, MA 02111.

Preventing Teen Dating Violence—Three Session Curriculum for Teaching Adolescents by C. Sousa, L. Bancroft, & T. German, 1991. Published by the Dating Violence Instruction Project, c/o Transition House, P.O. Box 530, Harvard Square Station, Cambridge, MA 02238.

The Prevention of Youth Violence: A Framework for Community Action by the Center for Environmental Health and Injury Control, Division of Injury Control at the Centers for Disease Control, 1992. This manual is designed to help reduce violence and prevent injuries and deaths from violence among youths in their community. It is based on principles of effective, community-based health promotion programs that address a variety of chronic diseases as well as problems of youth such as sexually transmitted diseases and teenage pregnancy. Published by Centers for Disease Control, Atlanta, GA.

Safe and Alive by Terry Dobson with Judith Shepard-Chow, 1981. This guide to protecting self and property contains a very clear and practical discussion of fight, flight, and other options. Dobson is a martial arts expert. Published by J.P. Tarcher, Los Angeles.

Safe Passage on City Streets by Dorothy T. Samuel, 1975. An optimistic and easy-to-read book of experiences in which people have countered violence with non-violence—good for use with students. Published by Abingdon Press, Nashville, TN.

School Safety and Security Management. Published by Rusting Publications, 403 Main Street, Port Washington, NY 11050 (516) 883-1440.

School Safety World. Published by National Safety Council, 444 North Michigan Avenue, Chicago, IL 60601.

School Safety Check Book, 1990. Published by National School Safety Center, Malibu, CA.

School Safety Journal and National School Safety Center Report. This periodical offers timely information on school violence prevention efforts around the nation. Published by the National School Safety Center, 4165 Thousand Oaks Boulevard, Suite 290, Westlake Village, CA 91362 (818) 377-6200.

Second Step: A Violence Prevention Curriculum. This curriculum is designed for grades 1–3, 4–5, and 6–8. Published by Committee for Children, 172 20th Avenue, Seattle, WA 98122 (206) 322-5050.

Set Straight on Bullies by S. Greenbaum, B. Turner, and R. D. Stephens, 1989. This resource contains valuable information about what causes children to become bullies, the harm they can cause to other children, and ways to reduce this damaging phenomenon. Published by National School Safety Center, Malibu, CA.

Special Focus. Preventing Violence: Program Ideas and Examples, 1992. This booklet presents a cross-section of anti-violence programs representing a broad spectrum of partners, audiences, and long- and short-term efforts to address violence concerns in communities. Published by the National Crime Prevention Council, Washington, DC.

Violence and Aggression by Ronald H. Bailey, 1976. An excellent and readable summary of research in the area. Its use of illustrations make it a good resource for students as well. Published by Time-Life Books, New York.

Violence Prevention: Curriculum for Adolescents by Deborah Prothrow-Stith, 1987. This curriculum guide contains sample lessons, exercises, projects, and handouts to help teachers and students address the issues of violence. Its goal is to help students become more aware of positive ways to deal with anger and arguments, how fights begin and escalate, and non-violent choices for conflict situations. A set of sixteen handouts is included. Published by Education Development Center, Incorporated, 55 Chapel Street, Newton, MA 02160.

Who's Hurt and Who's Liable? Sexual Harassment in Massachusetts Schools. A Curriculum and Guide for School Personnel, by F. Klein and N. Wilber, 1986. A curriculum and guide for all members of the school community, this publication defines sexual harassment, explains the legal issues involved, describes administrative strategies, and presents student activities and classroom lessons in the subject. Published by the Massachusetts Department of Education, 1385 Hancock Street, Quincy, MA 02169.

Additional Resources

by Stephanie Kadel and Joseph Follman

American Bar Association
Standing Committee on Dispute Resolution
2nd Floor South
1800 M Street NW
Washington, DC 20036
(202) 331-2258

American Association of Retired Persons
Criminal Justice Services
601 E Street, NW
Building B, Fifth Floor
Washington, DC 20049
(202) 728-4363

American Association of School Administrators
1801 North Moore Street
Arlington, VA 22209
(703) 528-0700

Center for Research on Aggression
Syracuse University
805 South Crouse Avenue
Syracuse, NY 13244-2280
(315) 443-9641

Office of School Safety
New York City Board of Education
600 E. 6th Street
New York, NY 10009
(212) 979-3300

From *Hot Topics: Usable Research, Reducing School Violence*, the SouthEastern
Regional Vision for Education, 1993, p. 73–74. Reprinted with permission.

Community Guidance Clinic
Trent and Elva Streets
Durham, NC 27705
(919) 684-3044

Community Relations Service
U.S. Department of Justice
5550 Friendship Boulevard
Suite 330
Chevy Chase, MD 20815
(301) 492-5929

Division of Injury Control
National Center for Injury Prevention and Control
Centers for Disease Control
4770 Buford Highway, NE
Atlanta, GA 30348
(404) 488-4690

Education Development Center, Inc.
55 Chapel Street
Newton, MA 02160
(617) 969-7100

I Am Somebody, Period, Inc.
851 Pinewell Drive
Cincinnati, OH 45255
(513) 474-4449

Judge Baker Guidance Center
295 Longwood Avenue
Boston, MA 02115
(617) 232-8390

National Alliance for Safe Schools
4903 Edgemoor Lane
Suite 403
Bethesda, MA 20814
(301) 654-2774

National Assault Prevention Center
Post Office Box 02005
Columbus, OH 43202
(614) 291-2540

National Association of Elementary School Principals
1615 Duke Street
Alexandria, VA 22314-3483
(703) 684-3345

National Association of Secondary School Principals
1904 Association Drive
Reston, VA 22091-1598
(703) 860-0200

National Center for the Study of Corporal
Punishment and Alternatives in the Schools
253 Ritter Annex
Temple University
Philadelphia, PA 19122
(215) 787-6091

National Crime Prevention Council
1700 K Street
Washington, DC 20006
(202) 466-6272

National Crime Prevention Institute
Brigman Hall
University of Louisville
Louisville, KY 40292
(502) 588-6987

National Committee for the Prevention of Child Abuse
332 South Michigan Avenue
Suite 1600
Chicago, IL 60604-3817
(312) 633-3520

National Exchange Clubs Foundation for the Prevention of Child Abuse
3050 Central Avenue
Toledo, OH 43606
(419) 535-3232

National McGruff House Network
1879 South Main, Suite 180
Salt Lake City, UT 84115
(801) 486-8768

National Organization for Victim Assistance
1757 Park Road, NW
Washington, DC 20010
(202) 232-6682

The National PTA
700 North Rush Street
Chicago, IL 60611-2571
(312) 787-0977

National School Boards Association
1680 Duke Street
Alexandria, VA 22314
(703) 838-6760

National School Safety Center
4165 Thousand Oaks Boulevard
Suite 290
Westlake Village, CA 91362
(805) 373-9977

National Urban League, Inc.
Stop the Violence Clearinghouse
500 East 62nd Street
New York, NY 10021
(212) 310-9000

National Victim Center
309 West 7th Street, Suite 705
Fort Worth, TX 76102
(817) 877-3355

Natural Helpers (Peer Counseling)
Roberts, Fitzmahan and Associates
9131 California Avenue, SW
Seattle, WA 98136-2599
(206) 932-8409

Prevention Intervention Program in Trauma, Violence and
Sudden Bereavement in Childhood
Dr. Robert S. Pynoos, Director
UCLA Department of Psychiatry and Biobehavioral Sciences
750 Westwood Plaza
Los Angeles, CA 90024
(310) 206-8973

Prince George County Public Schools
Peter Blauvelt, Director of Security
507 Largo Road
Upper Marlboro, MD 20722
(301) 336-5400

Society for the Prevention of Violence
3109 Mayfield Road
Room 207
Cleveland Heights, OH 44118
(216) 371-5545

REFERENCES

Bastian, L.D., & Taylor, B.M. (1991). *School Crime: A national crime victimization survey report.* Washington, DC: U.S. Department of Justice.

Bodinger-DeUriarte, C., & Sancho, A.R. (1992). *Hate crime: Sourcebook for
schools.* Los Alamitos, CA: Southwest Regional Laboratory, and Philadelphia: Research for Better Schools.

McMahon, E.T., Zimmer, J.A., Modglin, T.W., & O'Neil, J.F. (1988). *Teens, crime, and the community: Education and action for safer schools and neighborhoods.* St. Paul, MN: West Publishing Company.

National School Safety Center. (1989). *Student and staff victimization.* Malibu, CA: Author.

National School Safety Center. (1990a). *School crisis prevention and response.* Malibu, CA: Author.

Prothrow-Stith, D. (1987). *Violence prevention: Curriculum for adolescents.* Newton, MA: Education Development Center.

Roderick, T. (1987, December–1988, January). Johnny can learn to negotiate. *Educational Leadership* 4, (45), 86–90.

Stop the violence: Start something. (1991). Washington, DC: National Crime Prevention Council.

Authors

Richard F. Arthur has been a school board member, a high school principal, a CETA administrator, a high school and adult school counselor, a supervisor of student teachers, an assistant professor of education, and a teacher.

Joseph Beckham is chairman of the Department of Educational Leadership, Florida State University.

Wally Bowen teaches media literacy at the North Carolina Center for the Advancement of Teaching and also at the University of North Carolina at Chapel Hill's Principals' Executive Program. He is also the executive director of Citizens for Media Literacy, which is based in Asheville, NC.

Carter Burns is associate chair of the Division of Administration, Teacher Education, and Industrial Technology, Teachers College, Emporia State University, Emporia, Kansas.

Mary Lynn Cantrell is the Director of Training and Evaluation for the Positive Education Process and past president of the American Re-Education Association.

Susan E. Craig is special projects coordinator at AGH Associates, Inc., Hampton, NH.

Thomas W. Fleming is a police officer with the Park Forest Police Department and is a police liaison counselor at Rich East High School.

Joseph Follman is Director of Publications for SouthEastern Regional Vision for Education.

Gus Frias, a former Los Angeles police officer, is currently a member of the Advisory Committee on School Violence for the California Commission on Teacher Credentialing and a technical expert for the National School Safety Center.

David Frisby is a lieutenant in the Tallahassee (FL) Police Department, and a former high school teacher and member of Florida Criminal Justice Standards and Training Curriculum Subcommittee.

Donna Harrington-Lueker is an associate editor of *The Executive Editor.*

Stephanie Kadel is a research assistant for SouthEastern Regional Vision for Education.

Walt Landen, a political science major with secondary education minor at Randolph-Macon College, Ashland, Virginia, served as an intern at NSBA. (Karen Powe contributed to his article.)

Anthony Moriarty is assistant principal at Rich East High School in Park Forest, IL, and a licensed clinical psychologist in private practice.

Mary Nebgen, formerly deputy superintendent of the Tacoma public schools, is superintendent of the Washoe County, NE public schools.

Pat Ordovensky, former education writer for U.S.A. Today, is a freelance writer in Sarasota, FL.

Sara Podell is an English teacher at Morton West High School in Berwyn, IL and an educational researcher and freelance writer.

Jessica Portner is a reporter and writer for Education Week in Washington, DC.

Marc Posner conducts research in health promotion and risk prevention at the Education Development Center in Newton, MA.

Peter Schmidt, formerly with *The Associated Press*, has been a staff writer at *Education Week* for five years.

Philip Stelly is a freelance writer living in New Orleans.

Kenneth S. Trump is coordinator of the Youth Gang Unit of the Cleveland Public Schools and an independent consultant on youth violence, gangs, and school security.

Debra L. Williams is associate editor of *Catalyst*, a monthly publication of the Community Renewal Society that is documenting school reform in Chicago.

Acknowledgments

Grateful acknowledgment is made to the following authors and agents for their permission to reprint copyrighted materials.

Section 2
The SouthEastern Regional Vision for Education (SERVE) for *Hot Topics: Usable Research, Reducing School Violence* by Stephanie Kadel and Joseph Follman, p. vii. Reprinted with permission. Copyright © 1993 SouthEastern Regional Vision for Education. All rights reserved.

Education Week for "Educators Keeping Eye on Measures Designed to Combat Youth Violence" by Jessica Portner. Vol. 13, no. 20, p. 21, Feb. 9, 1994. Reprinted with permission. Copyright © 1994 Editorial Projects in Education. All rights reserved.

The Executive Educator for "Youth Gangs Aren't Just a Big City Problem" by Anthony Moriarty and Thomas W. Fleming. Vol. 12, no. 7, p. 13–16, July 1990. Reprinted with permission. Copyright © 1990 the National School Boards Association. All rights reserved.

Education Week for "Media Violence" by Wally Bowen. Vol. 13, no. 25, p. 60, 47, March 9, 1994. Reprinted with permission. Copyright © 1994 Editorial Projects in Education. All rights reserved.

The SouthEastern Regional Vision for Education (SERVE) for *Hot Topics: Usable Research, Reducing School Violence* by Stephanie Kadel and Joseph Follman, p. 61–64. Reprinted with permission. Copyright © 1993 SouthEastern Regional Vision for Education. All rights reserved.

Section 3
The SouthEastern Regional Vision for Education (SERVE) for *Hot Topics: Usable Research, Reducing School Violence* by Stephanie Kadel and Joseph Follman, p. 21–47. Reprinted with permission. Copyright © 1993 SouthEastern Regional Vision for Education. All rights reserved.

The National Education Service for "What Can We Do About Gangs" by Mary Lynn Cantrell. From the *Journal of Emotional and Behavioral Problems: Reclaiming Children and Youth* vol. 1, no. 1, p. 34–37, Spring 1992. Reprinted

Section 4

The American School Board Journal for "Safe Streets in Tacoma" by Mary Nebgen. vol. 177, no. 10, p. 26–27, October 1990. Reprinted with permission. Copyright © 1990 the National School Boards Association. All rights reserved.

The American School Board Journal for "Tell Teen Gangs: School's Out" by Kenneth S. Trump. vol. 180, no. 7, p. 39–42, July 1993. Reprinted with permission. Copyright © 1993 the National School Boards Association. All rights reserved.

Education Week for "Age of Reckoning" by Peter Schmidt. vol. 13, no. 24, p. 24–27, March 9, 1994. Reprinted with permission. Copyright © 1994 Editorial Projects in Education. All rights reserved.

The American School Board Journal for "Okaying the use of metal detectors proves easier than actually using them" by Philip Stelly. vol. 171, no. 3, p. 47, March 1984. Reprinted with permission. Copyright © 1984 the National School Boards Association. All rights reserved.

Sara Podell for "Confronting the Crisis in the Criminal Justice System" by Sara Podell. From the *Technical Assistance Bulletin*, no. 5, published by the American Bar Association. Reprinted with permission. Copyright © 1992 Sara Podell. All rights reserved.

The Harvard Graduate School of Education for "We Need a National Strategy for Safe Schools" by Gus Frias. From *The Harvard Education Newsletter* vol. X, no. 3, p. 4–5, May/June 1994. Reprinted with permission. Copyright © 1994 by the President and Fellows of Harvard College. All rights reserved.

Section 5
The SouthEastern Regional Vision for Education (SERVE) for *Hot Topics: Usable Research, Reducing School Violence* by Stephanie Kadel and Joseph Follman, p. 67–74. Reprinted with permission. Copyright © 1993 SouthEastern Regional Vision for Education. All rights reserved.

Index

There are
one-story intellects,
two-story intellects, and three-story
intellects with skylights. All fact collectors, who have
no aim beyond their facts, are one-story men. Two-story men compare,
reason, generalize, using the labors of the fact collectors as well as their
own. Three-story men idealize, imagine, predict—
their best illumination comes from
above, through the skylight.
—*Oliver Wendell*
Holmes